"This book recalls for us the fundamental motives that led, with great effort, to the liturgical reforms of Vatican II. It is a timely reminder of forgotten truths of the liturgical movement, namely, that it was and is a question not only of reforming the liturgical books but of forming Christians themselves through profound and conscious participation in the liturgical rites and prayers. It provides conceptual tools for a deep theological consideration of the intentions of the reform as well as a way of confronting the theological questions that necessary emerge from Benedict XVI's motu proprio *Summorum Pontificum*."

—Jeremy Driscoll, OSB
Pontifical Athenaeum Sant' Anselmo
Mount Angel Seminary

"Andrea Grillo advances the debate on the liturgical reform with definitive evidence: despite the conflict of interpretations on *Sacrosanctum Concilium* and the motu proprio *Summorum Pontificum* of 2007, the theology of the liturgy of Vatican II remains a key part of the great and irrepressible reformulation of the church's understanding of itself at Vatican II."

—Massimo Faggioli
University of St. Thomas

"In these five short but passionately written chapters, Andrea Grillo emphasizes how urgent it is to transcend the paralyzing polemics of recent years, provoked by reform of the liturgy, and to face with openness and determination the more fundamental but forgotten or as-yet-unknown aspects of the liturgical vision of Vatican II and of the early twentieth-century thinkers whose amazing insights prepared for it without intending to do so.

"Barry Hudock deserves commendation for introducing one of Italy's most prolific and highly respected theologians to the English-speaking world in such a clear and readable translation."

—Patrick Regan, OSB
Professor Emeritus, Pontificio
Ateneo Sant' Anselmo

D1528929

Andrea Grillo

Beyond Pius V

*Conflicting Interpretations
of the Liturgical Reform*

Translated by Barry Hudock

Revised Edition

A PUEBLO BOOK

Liturgical Press   Collegeville, Minnesota
www.litpress.org

A Pueblo Book published by Liturgical Press

Cover design by Jodi Hendrickson. Cover image: Wikipedia.

This book was originally published as *Oltre Pio V. La riforma liturgica nel conflitto di interpretazioni*, © 2007 by Editrice Queriniana, Brescia, Italy.

1	2	3	4	5	6	7	8	9

Library of Congress Cataloging-in-Publication Data

Grillo, Andrea.
    [Oltre Pio V. English]
    Beyond Pius V : conflicting interpretations of the liturgical reform / Andrea Grillo ; translated by Barry Hudock. — Revised Edition.
      pages cm
    "A Pueblo book."
    Includes bibliographical references.
    ISBN 978-0-8146-6302-8 — ISBN 978-0-8146-6327-1 (ebook)
    1. Liturgical reform.   2. Liturgical movement—Catholic Church.   3. Catholic Church—Liturgy—History—20th century.   I. Title.

BX1975.G7513   2013
264'.02—dc2   2013031501

To the great-grandparents and
    great-grandchildren
of the liturgical reform:
that those who are no longer with us,
in communion with those who are not yet
    with us,
may teach us
not only the *unum necessarium*
but also the *quod superest*.

Contents

Chapter 5
Liturgical Reform and Virtual Reality:
Benedict XVI's Motu Proprio *Summorum Pontificum*
and the Ecclesia Dei Commission's Instruction
Universae Ecclesiae 94

Preface to the American Edition

More than five years after it was first published in Italian, *Beyond Pius V* now appears in English. The first Italian edition was published in May 2007, two months before the promulgation of Pope Benedict XVI's motu proprio *Summorum Pontificum*, based on hints and rumors about the coming document that had been circulating through Rome for many months. Now, with the hindsight of five years, it seemed necessary to update the text. The first four chapters here remain the same, with the exception of some minor revisions, and I have added a completely new fifth chapter, commenting on *Summorum Pontificum* (July 7, 2007) and the Ecclesia Dei Commission's instruction, *Universae Ecclesiae* (April 30, 2011). These two documents offer ample and objective confirmation of the concerns I raised in my original text. They make clear the need for an adequate hermeneutic of the Second Vatican Council and of the liturgical reform, to which theology can and must make an important contribution.

This book contributes to a discussion already in progress in the American context, particularly in two notable and recently published works. Massimo Faggioli's *True Reform: Liturgy and Ecclesiology in* Sacrosanctum Concilium and Patrick Regan's skillful historical and theological study, *Advent to Pentecost: Comparing the Seasons in the Ordinary and Extraordinary Forms of the Roman Rite*, both offer important scholarly evidence that the Catholic Church of the third millenium ought to understand itself not "according to Pius V" or "against Pius V" but decidedly "beyond Pius V." The fact that the same publisher now follows these two books with this English version of my own is surely a "sign of the times" worth noting.

Andrea Grillo
Rome
November 9, 2012
Dedication of the Lateran Basilica

Introduction

Nothing can ever happen twice.
In consequence, the sorry fact is
that we arrive here improvised
and leave without the chance to practice.

W. Szymborska[1]

The reform of the liturgy is at risk. Indeed, at least in its most authentic and prophetic aspects, it now seems to be widely *ignored*. Various developments, sometimes quite troubling, have sown doubts and confusion within the ecclesial community. The restoration of the Missal of Pius V and "liberalization" of the use of the preconciliar rite, demands from the highest levels for the use of a "dead" language, irresponsible and superficial comments offered publicly by important officials of the Roman Curia, unjustified crackdowns on the work of translators, an inversion of priorities between mystery and discipline, never-ending lists of abuses, and a dangerous disregard for the meaning of liturgical "uses": these are only some of the signs of the serious threat that faces the ideas that have inspired and sustained the liturgical reform for nearly fifty years.

[1] [From the poem "Nothing Twice," by Nobel Prize–winning poet Wisława Szymborska; English translation (ET) in Wisława Szymborska, *Poems New and Collected: 1957–1997* (New York: Harcourt, 1998), 20.—Trans.]

While church authorities certainly pay attention to liturgy, their interventions—despite formal references to all the right documents—are "out of tune" with the foundational reasons for the reform. At the same time, it can be said that the quality of reflection carried on from "the other side" has also been inconsistent. "Historical" arguments—frequently positivistic in nature—are too often treated as the only kind that is legitimate or admissible.

The entire discussion is too often marked by biased presumptions, a sour nostalgia, and an antimodern and reactionary spirit, yet it is supported by surprisingly modern and ultraliberal arguments. It will suffice to mention, by way of example, the broad reintroduction of the Missal of Pius V, justified by an appeal to a "freedom of rite" that is offered with disregard for the unwanted consequences that such a development might bring in its concrete application. What might appear on the face of it to be a masterstroke of moderation risks becoming, more likely, a solemn mess for which no one is held accountable.

We can say, in fact, that while it may be hard to find many effective or serious attempts to attack the liturgical reform directly, it is no less difficult today to find defenses of the reform that don't amount to pretty much the same thing. Indeed, if there are enemies of the liturgical reform to speak of, they rarely attack it head-on. Instead—with cunning and more than a little wordplay—they prefer to weaken the very terrain on which the reform stands. *Reintroducing old meanings of "participation in the liturgy" or inventing new theories of "freedom of rite," these authors suggest that the need for reform is long past, downgrade it to merely one possibility among many, and so effectively overcome it.*

For this reason, it is urgent that the church today refresh its collective memory of the essential meaning of the liturgical reform. I suggest there are at least four dimensions of this task, each absolutely fundamental for the life of the church today and tomorrow. Neglecting them would mean allowing the very foundations of the reform to crumble.

First and before all else, the meaning and significance of the Second Vatican Council in the history of the church in the twentieth century must be clearly grasped. Various reductive readings of Vatican II acknowledge only the "continuity" of that Council and its documents while completely ignoring their *profoundly innovative aspects, the developments and changes that can be seen only with difficulty as a pure continuation of recent ecclesial tradition.* This contraposition between hermeneutic of reform and hermeneutic of discontinuity, authoritatively proposed as the authentic interpretation of the Council, bears a certain ideological character, especially in the way it dismisses the differences between "before" and "after," for fear of acknowledging the slightest discontinuity.

Second, the key concept of "active participation"—as the true objective to which the entire liturgical reform was oriented and the fundamental motive that continues to nourish it—deserves a profound reconsideration today, especially because it is now often disregarded in favor of ideas that are proposed and received initially to great effect but are unable, in the long run, to bear the weight of common sense. *The participation of the entire assembly in the single liturgical action is the fundamental purpose of the reform.* If we forget the clarity and centrality of this decisive fact, the reform itself is rendered superfluous, almost effortlessly.

Third, we must *thoroughly reconsider the themes of the early liturgical movement* in order to understand how it played such a decisive role, not only before, but also during and after the reform of the liturgy. This will make it possible to identify above all in this "first" liturgical movement—which extends from the end of the 1800s to the 1950s—a surprising focus not primarily on liturgical reform but on the movement's "participative" and "formative" intentions.

Finally, it is essential that we distinguish between, on the one hand, what the liturgical reform could and still can do and, on the other, what it had to and still must discover about itself in the work of the generations that preceded and followed it. This conclusion should help to explain the tension between reformative act and formative act in light of the concrete liturgical experience of the church.

A thorough consideration of these problems and themes will provide the essential foundation for a contemporary rereading of the great reformative phase through which the Catholic liturgy has passed in the past fifty years. This is the task of the little book I offer here. I hope to clarify (for myself and for my readers) the prophetic and unsurpassed meaning of the period we have come to call the liturgical reform, which constitutes—in the context established by the Council's magisterium—a "beginning of a beginning" (K. Rahner). We can appropriately explore this meaning in only one way: by responsibly receiving the gift that has been handed on to us and discovering in it our particular task, which is not in all ways the same as that of those who came before us.

Perhaps what is most lacking today is a strong awareness of this generational and pedagogical dimension of the Second Vatican Council, which was even then aware of being in need of "children and grandchildren" so that the tradition might have a future and so that it could therefore consider its own *munus* to be not simply the continuation of a *traditum* but the "beginning of a beginning"—never claiming a "beginning *ex novo*," obviously, but also never presuming to be a continuation completely as before.

The conflict of interpretations in liturgical matters that dangerously marks the life of the church today exists in large part because this authentic traditional concern "for the children and grandchildren" has been forgotten. We can recover it today by rediscovering accurately the principles that guided the original liturgical movement and the liturgical reform: that the Christian liturgy can still "generate faith" and can still be the *fons* of the church's life and of personal spirituality. This was the singular hope and objective of the reform, and we may not ignore or dismiss it. It will continue to challenge and provoke us, provided that we have not decided—desperately and boastfully—that we are the last Christians, faithful to a great and (merely) ancient tradition, which we have reduced to a precious past closed up in a museum, with air conditioning and security systems but without life and without children.

Chapter 1

Vatican II and the "New Forms" of the Primacy of Mystery

> Yes, the Church of the council has been con-
> cerned, not just with herself and with her rela-
> tionship of union with God, but with man—man
> as he really is today: living man, man all wrapped
> up in himself, man who makes himself not only
> the center of his every interest but dares to claim
> that he is the principle and explanation of all real-
> ity. *Every perceptible element in man* . . . has, in a
> sense, been displayed in full view of the council
> Fathers.[1]

Reconstructing the authentic meaning of the liturgical reform and offering an accurate hermeneutic demands that we first recover the historical and ecclesial
context from which the liturgical movement—of which
we are all the children and grandchildren—emerged.
It is a task we must approach serenely, without anxiety
or hesitation, without remorse or regrets.

The Second Vatican Council was, in effect, an occasion on which the Catholic Church profoundly *rethought*
its own identity, its own relationship with itself and

---

[1] Pope Paul VI, Address during the Last General Meeting of the
Second Vatican Council, 7 December 1965, italics mine [ET: http://
www.vatican.va/holy_father /paul_vi/speeches/1965/documents
/hf_p-vi_spe_19651207_epilogo-concilio_en.html.—Trans.].

with the world. Fifty years later, we need to *think again about this rethinking*, aware, in doing so, not only that the Council becomes the *object* of our study but also that we must know how to continue to receive it as a *subject* able to rouse the mind, enflame the heart, and give a new vitality to the body.[2]

In speaking here of the body, we mean not only the mind and the heart, since our own bodies and the body of the church meet and are gathered up in the Body of Christ, where they come together as one. Therefore, it is from the body—from my own living body—that I start, beginning my reflections on an autobiographical note, as discussion of the Council so often does. Many who reflect on the Council do so with great excitement and emotion, noting the connections between their own lives and the Council, between their bodily age and the events of Vatican II: "When I was sixteen years old . . ."; "When I visited Rome . . ."; "When I saw the altar turned around for the first time . . ."; and the like.

For me, the Second Vatican Council is a bit like my baptism: having been born in 1961, I lived it before I was aware of it. For me, and for all Catholics born in the past fifty years, the Council is simply the ecclesial context upon which the story of our lives—our bodies,

---

[2] It is therefore useful to recall that "our" rethinking risks much (or, one might say, risks everything) if we forget the rethinking that has already happened and that we are living. Otherwise we can easily fall into the danger and the temptation of reducing the Council to our criteria of understanding, thereby losing much of the specificity of the *conciliar method*, which consists not so much in changing the "objects" of ecclesial attention as changing the *forms of life* through which these objects are experienced and expressed!

our hearts, and our minds—is written. This is truly the strength of the tradition, and it should not surprise us; indeed, it compels us to discover that for younger generations a different principle prevails than for those who preceded them: for them, the Council is—unavoidably and providentially—a historical event. They can and must "rethink" the Council, but they never faced the considerable challenge of "thinking it" for the first time, at the beginning. Our ability to *rethink* it, therefore, presupposes that others before us *thought the Council, without us but for us and in a sense with us in mind, in the hope that we might have the benefit of a new perspective, another way of approaching and understanding the church and the world, the human person and God.*

In going about this rethinking *apres coup*, these new generations—those who are not "fathers" or "brothers" of the Council but rather its children—will necessarily have new questions, different needs, sometimes different or even opposite priorities. For this reason, I want briefly to consider three questions. First, what does it mean for new generations of Christians to rethink the Council? Second, what is implied by the fact that this rethinking involves not only the content but also the very experience of faith? And finally, what can all of this tell us about both the "anthropological question" and the "liturgical question," which stand at the heart of contemporary theological reflection, that will help us understand and recover the conciliar approach as we consider the reception of the liturgical reform in today's context?

1. THE SECOND VATICAN COUNCIL AND OPENNESS TO THE OTHER: A QUESTION OF METHOD

It is often rightly said that the Second Vatican Council brought about within the Catholic Church a new attitude of *openness* to the world and to modern society. This openness is expressed clearly in the constitution *Gaudium et Spes*, but it also marks the other three conciliar constitutions, *Sacrosanctum Concilium*, *Lumen Gentium*, and *Dei Verbum*. Taking into consideration all four documents not only offers richer content for reflection on this topic but, more importantly, also suggests *a decisive methodological choice.*

In effect, the Council made a crucial rediscovery (though it did so initially without being completely aware of it—in some ways anticipating its intentions and its *"mens"* by its method of deliberation and its actions): *revelation and faith can be experienced in many ways and by many paths.* The Council refused to be frightened away from this plurality or to seek easy forms of *reductio ad unum.* Rather, it chose to travel the way of *four different paths* that, while arriving at the same point, follow different routes and disclose different horizons.

For this reason, to truly rethink Vatican II means first of all to reconsider, modify, and correct an understanding of its "teaching" that is too simple and too linear.[3] The anthropology that emerges from the

---

[3] Cf. G. Colombo, "Vaticano II e postoconcilio. Uno sguardo retrospettivo," *La Scuola Cattolica*, 133 (2005): 3–18; A. Melloni, *Chiesa madre, chiesa matrigna. Un discorso storico sul cristianesimo che cambia*, Vele 12 (Torino: Einaudi, 2004); G. Routhier, "A 40 anni dal Concilio Vaticano II. Un lungo tirocinio verso un nuovo tipo di catto-

Council is not limited to what is found in *Gaudium et Spes*. There is also much to glean from *Sacrosanctum Concilium*, *Dei Verbum*, and *Lumen Gentium*. Indeed, we can say that while *Gaudium et Spes* appears at first glance to be the document most "advanced" in its anthropology, its approach is the most linear and the least nuanced, since it employs a communicative style by which new ideas are presented in a classical form (that is, in a style drawn from the theological-philosophical tradition of the previous two centuries). On the other hand, the documents that might seem to be imbued with a less theoretically elaborate approach (*Sacrosanctum Concilium* or *Dei Verbum*) are anthropologically (and therefore theologically) far more provocative, because they repropose more "classical" ideas, but they do it in a *renewed form*. They affirm, in substance, that a definition of the human person, a metaphysics of being, and even a doctrine of mystery are not enough but that we must begin from even more *fundamental* (which is not to say less challenging or demanding) *data*: hearing the word, the celebration of rite, the lived relationships of ecclesial communion. These "forms of Christian life" merit priority of attention. For the anthropological question, still today, they emerge as the more radical and more decisive challenges.

---

licesimo," *La Scuola Cattolica*, 133 (2005): 19–52; Servizio Nazionale per il Progetto Culturale della CEI, *A quarant'anni dal Concilio. VI Forum del Progetto Culturale* (Bologna: EDB, 2005). More recently, two volumes are indispensible in reconstructing the history of the Council: Christoph Théobald, *La recezione del Vaticano II. I. Tornare alla sorgente* (Bologna: EDB, 2011), and John W. O'Malley, *What Happened at Vatican II?* (Cambridge, MA: Belknap Press, 2008).

2. "EVERY PERCEPTIBLE ELEMENT IN MAN" AND THE PERSISTENT TEMPTATION OF FORMALISTIC REDUCTION

As we have seen, the great project of the Council offers us not so much new articles of faith but a new methodological approach to the *forms of life* and *fundamental experiences* by way of which the church is united symbolically to its Lord. It is clear from this that the Council cannot be understood (or rethought) by substituting its particular method with another method or approach, and certainly not with the one that the Council specifically intended to move beyond.

To explain this idea more clearly, I offer two brief examples:

First, with regard to the relationship between reason and faith, there is no question that one thing necessary today is a renewed effort at research into the accessibility/plausibility of faith. An essential aspect of this exploration must be a conception of "reason" that acknowledges the ways that symbol, rite, and language "give rise to thought" (P. Ricoeur). It is important to resist the temptation of *reducing* experience to a monological and self-sufficient idea, which tries to answer the anthropological question without a willingness to take up the task of following *the long way* toward the authoritative word, the ritual symbol, and ecclesial communion. Here, frankly, the human and natural sciences not only are not "suspect"; what is extremely suspect is any attempt to get along without them.

Second, regarding an understanding of mystery, it is important today that a metaphysics of being and a doctrine of mystery are properly understood. While it is tempting to begin with a metaphysical or doctrinal definition of mystery, we must remember that the

Council asked us to understand "mystery" not only as an *enigma* or a *secret*, and not only as a *truth to be known*, but above all as *word* to hear and to proclaim, as *sacrament* to be celebrated and in which to participate, as *church* to live within and to love. What are the four conciliar constitutions if not a great exploration and unfolding of mystery—the mystery of Christ and of the church—not only on the doctrinal and intellectual level, but also in the symbolic corporeity of a rite, in the lucid obedience to a word, and in the articulated form of ecclesial relationships? I believe that if we insist on holding fast to recognizing only a strictly doctrinalistic definition of mystery in the teaching of the Council, not only will we be unable to rethink the Council accurately, but we risk convincing ourselves (and persuading others) that it was substantially *superfluous*.

3. THE LITURGICAL QUESTION BETWEEN ANTHROPOLOGY AND THEOLOGY: A CONCILIAR SYNTHESIS THAT REMAINS UNDONE

One conclusion of all of this must be a reformulation of the "liturgical question" that—following the conciliar methodology—takes into account all fields of knowledge. And this has not happened yet. It represents a response to a deep purpose, which must be expressed in rich and varied ways. It is the irrepressible drive for a "first philosophy" that is supported—and not threatened—by exteriority aimed at achieving interiority, by the institution reaching for spontaneity, by grace to recognize oneself as given in and to freedom.

We need to rediscover today the delicate and vital contribution of authoritative exteriority, of one's body and the body of another. For this reason, even the most unrelated sciences can prove to be not only helpful but even decisive for coming to a careful and thorough understanding of the structure and interrelatedness of the worshiping body, the confessing heart, and the believing intellect. An adequate elaboration of these relations would be able to show—among the fundamental preoccupations of both the liturgical movement and the Second Vatican Council—the need for a new understanding of the experience of faith that that holds together internal and external, *"ratio et manus"* (T. Aquinas), brain, mouth, and hand (G. Lafont).

Nevertheless, this taking up of a symbolic-ritual, scriptural, and ecclesial body is not identified with either that which is public or that which is private. It is rather the communitarian and intersubjective dimension—more than subjective and more than objective—to establish here the new point of departure, even for the contemporary "anthropological question," in order to overcome the disfiguring absolutism of both sentimental freedom and political authority, and to obtain that felt and liberating authority that faith cannot fail to preserve, discreetly and, one might almost say, modestly.

But this discretion and modesty are the fruits of a great passion, stirred up by an accurate understanding of history. We find an example of this in a passage of Bernanos's *The Diary of a Country Priest* when the curate of Torcy remembers *Rerum Novarum* in the same way we ought to remember the entire Second Vatican Council:

> For instance, that famous encyclical of Leo XIII, "Rerum Novarum," *you* can read that without turning a hair, like any instruction for keeping Lent. But when it was published, sonny, it was like an earth-

quake. The enthusiasm! At that time I was curé de Norenfontes, in the heart of the mining district. The simple notion that a man's work is not a commodity, subject to the law of supply and demand, that you have no right to speculate on wages, on the lives of men, as you do on grain, sugar, or coffee—why it set people's consciences upside down![4]

Only when we can once again feel the earth trembling under our feet and our consciences being turned upside down—this time by the central affirmations of the Council—can we think meaningfully again about Vatican II, about its great and irrepressible reformulation of the church's understanding of itself, and, above all, about the great mystery that pervades its origins and carries it faithfully through time.

All of this demands an inevitable reconsideration of the way that the *receptio* of the Council has in fact distorted the meaning of some of the most basic intentions of the Council itself.[5] Regarding liturgy, we must carefully assess the responses offered to the "liturgical

[4] The brilliant presentation of this citation from Bernanos is found in E. Benvenuto, *Il lieto annuncio ai poveri* (Bologna: EDB, 1997), 51. [ET: Georges Bernanos, *The Diary of a Country Priest* (New York: Macmillan, 1937), 57.—Trans.]

[5] Some interesting consequences of the conciliar period, often quite different from the original intentions, include:
   a) the "traditionalistic" effect of liturgical reform: the reform's concentration on "data about the past" has generated an exaltation of the past that has brought a rebirth of traditionalism today
   b) the "holy alliance" between Vatican I and Vatican II (and between them, the introduction of the Code of Canon Law): the union of the institutional centralization of the first council with the extraordinary decentralization backed by the second

question," which relate first of all to the recovery of the key concept of *actuosa participatio* and which have been marked at times by both progress and regression.[6] There has been significant difficulty surrounding the term, in identifying exactly what it ought to mean in terms of ritual activity and spiritual experience and in overcoming the inertia of deep-rooted ecclesial habits and spiritual styles.

---

c) the change of the concept of "magisterium" from negative to positive, with some undesired effects: from the anathema, which was a protector of pluralism, to a "monist" absorption of every competency by a centralized authority

d) the subordination of the local community as true subject of the liturgy to higher levels of hierarchical activity, which has only been increased by a concentration in the media on the "Roman" aspect of ecclesial matters

On this topic, cf. A. Melloni, *Chiesa madre, chiesa matrigna*, 34–42.

[6] Cf. A Melloni, "*Sacrosanctum Concilium* 1963–2003: Lo spessore storico della Riforma Liturgica e la ricezione del Vaticano II," *Rivista Liturgica* 90 (2003): 915–30.

Chapter 2

The Question of Active Participation, from Pius Parsch to *Redemptionis Sacramentum*

> The liturgical movement first had a restorative phase (Solesmes); then an academic phase (Maria Laach, Beuron); and finally a realistic phase (Rothenfels, Oratory of Lipsia, Klosterneuburg).
>
> —R. Guardini[1]

The urgent need for an adequate response to the liturgical question—left unresolved by a reform of the rites alone—and the powerful reemergence today of the *vexata quaestio* of "active participation" loom large in any telling of the history of the liturgical movement. We stand within (not outside of) that history. If the liturgical reform is, in fact, fundamentally about returning the liturgy to its place as *fons et culmen* of the entire life of the church, then it was inevitable that the question of *practical ritual participation* would emerge at some point as a sort of litmus test for its effectiveness.[2]

---

[1] Romano Guardini, diary entry for May 26, 1953.

[2] For a careful evaluation of the liturgical movement and questions of its theological understanding of the liturgy, these recent works make strong contributions: M. Pajano, *Liturgia e società nel novecento. percorsi del movimento liturgico di fronte ai processi di secolarizzazione*, Biblioteca di storia sociale 28 (Rome: Edizioni di Storia

To approach our topic adequately, we must first step back a century—prior to the fifty years that have followed the promulgation of *Sacrosanctum Concilium*,[3] and then back still further, another fifty years, to the first decades of the twentieth century. In the 1920s, Father Agostino Gemelli, one of the most respected figures in the church of his time, "discovered" Pius Parsch through the activities of L'Opera della Regalà[4] and, with his characteristic impetuous-

e Letteratura, 2000); A. Angenendt, *Liturgik und Historik. Gab es eine organische Liturgie-Entwicklung?*, Quaestiones Disputatae 189 (Freiburg-Basel-Wien, 2001) [Italian edition: *Liturgia e storia. Lo "sviluppo organico" in questione* (Assisi: Cittadella, 2005)]; M. Klöckener and B. Kranemann, eds., *Liturgiereformen. Historische Studien zu einem bleibenden Grundzug des christlichen Gottesdienstes*, 2 vols. (Münster: Aschendorff, 2002); A. Grillo, *La nascita della liturgia nel XX secolo. Saggio sul rapporto tra Movimento Liturgico e (post-)Modernità* (Assisi: Cittadella, 2003).

[3] See A. Grillo, "40 anni prima e 40 anni dopo *Sacrosanctum Concilium*: Una 'considerazione inattuale' sulla attualità del Movimento Liturgico," *Ecclesia Orans* 21 (2004): 269–300.

[4] For an introduction to the relationship between the Opera della Regalità and Father Gemelli, see A. Lameri, *L'attività di promozione liturgica dell'Opera della Regalità (1931–1945). Contributo allo studio del Movimento Liturgico Italiano*, "Saggi" 3 (Milan: Edizioni O.R., 1992), esp. 57–69. [The Franciscan friar and scholar Agostino Gemelli (1878–1959) and Italian lay woman Armida Barelli (1882–1952) founded L'Opera della Regalità di Nostro Signore Gesù Cristo—The Work of the Kingship of Our Lord Jesus Christ—in 1929 to promote the spiritual development of lay men and women. Their effort was a response to the 1925 publication of Pope Pius XI's encyclical *Quas Primas*, which asserted the kingship of Christ over the world and established the liturgical feast of Christ the King. L'Opera is formally recognized today by the Italian conference of Catholic bishops. Gemelli was also the founder of the Catholic University of the Sacred Heart in Milan, now one of the

ness, introduced him to the Italian church. The two men had in common the experience of having been left stunned by the experience of World War II. Parsch is almost forgotten today, but some aspects of his work are worth rediscovering. It is certainly helpful in exploring the idea of active participation in the liturgy adequately. And so we approach the topic by way of this great precursor, known well to our grandparents but ignored and forgotten—for no reason—by us grandchildren.

As we will see below, a basic introduction to Parsch's thinking (sections 1 and 2) will suggest a few points that merit further exploration. These include Parsch's evaluation of Pope Pius XII's encyclical *Mediator Dei* (section 3); a comparison of the two different concepts of participation offered by *Mediator Dei* and *Sacrosanctum Concilium* (section 4); the attempt today to restore the old concept of participation, which the Council chose to move beyond (section 5) and which many now are trying to restore to the center of liturgical experience, as if nothing ever happened, as if there was no liturgical movement and the liturgical quesion was an invention of the liberal media, allowing them to dismiss, in the blink of an eye, the very reason for the liturgical reform.

---

largest Catholic universities in the world. Barelli's cause for canonization was opened in 1970, and she was declared Venerable by Pope Benedict XVI in 2007.—Trans.]

1. PARSCH ON ACTIVE PARTICIPATION AND BAPTISMAL PRIESTHOOD

Parsch's work shed new light on one important aspect of liturgy in a masterful way. He spoke of liturgy in terms of "popular liturgy," but never in the sense of bringing the high and almost exclusive contents of a difficult and sophisticated concept down to a more pedestrian level. On the contrary, his contribution was to recover the essential nature of the "action of the people" (*leiton-ergon*) in the liturgy. For Parsch, *liturgy* and *popular liturgy* were not two separate topics, as though the latter were almost a subcategory of the former. Rather, the two terms are *synonyms*. If liturgy means more than formalism, rubricism, and legalism, but rather is the church's public worship, then the only approach that guarantees a faithfulness to liturgical tradition is to recognize it as being marked by *a pastoral and popular character*. Contrary to the clerical understanding of liturgy that marked the life of the church in recent centuries,[5] Parsch insists we must realize again that a "liturgy reserved exclusively to the priests" cannot exist.[6]

This first aspect of the concept of liturgy inevitably leads to a powerful (we might even say explosive) rediscovery: if the Mass is "a drama in which the priest and the faithful are actors together,"[7] then active participation in the liturgy reflects—on a dogmatic level—

---

[5] Cf. P. Parsch, *Le renouveau liturgique au service de la paroisse. Sens et portée de la liturgie populaire* (Mulhouse: Ed. Salvator, 1950), 24–25 (German original: *Volksliturgie. Ihr Sinn und Umfang* [Würzburg, 1940]).

[6] Cf. Parsch, *Le renouveau liturgique*, 25.

[7] Ibid., 37.

a conception of the church and ecclesial structure for which the "universal priesthood" is a necessary and indispensable foundation. "This is not," Parsch wrote, "an emancipation or a revolt of the people against the ministerial priesthood; it is simply the return to an ancient collaboration of priest and people in the liturgy that existed from the beginning."[8]

Even if subsequent historical studies call for the revision of some of the liturgical movement's classic assumptions about the reasons for the decline in active participation,[9] Parsch's understanding of the nature and importance of the concept (understood along the lines of participation in a theatrical event) and his elucidation of the dogmatic and canonical bases on which it is founded remain significant contributions.

I limit myself here to pointing out a few fundamental aspects of this vision:[10]

a. The gathered assembly is a true "actor" of the liturgy whose presence is not simply "tolerated."

b. A truly living liturgy, which produces its normal effects, never happens independent of participation by the assembly.

c. This participation is a corollary of the dogma of the mystical body and the consequent dogma of the universal priesthood.

d. The Christian priesthood is only an image of the singular priesthood of Christ, which assumes "universal" form in the sacraments of baptism and confirmation and "ordered" form in the sacrament of orders.

[8] Ibid., 25.
[9] Cf. Angenendt, *Liturgia e storia*, passim.
[10] Parsch, *Le renouveau liturgique*, 39–48.

e. The faithful truly and sacerdotally offer the sacrifice of the New Covenant under the authority of the ordained minister.

This vision, in the context of Parsh's time and ecclesial culture, is striking for its clarity and rigor. It is rooted in Parsch's passion for pastoral theology that is both scriptural and liturgical and rooted in a particular concept of liturgy. We will now examine that concept briefly.

2. PARSCH ON PARTICIPATION IN THE LITURGY

In Parsch's view, attempts to "translate" the liturgical movement into a "popular" liturgical movement were wrongheaded, because the "popular" nature of the movement was part of its essential structure. Liturgy, he knew, is always an act of "the whole Christ, head and body," a fact officially recognized in Pius XII's *Mediator Dei*. Here we find an almost prophetic value in Parsch's theological work: he recovered a meaningful relationship between the "method" and "object," the form and content of liturgical studies.

The renewal of liturgical theology was the fruit of a long period of important philological, historical, archaeological, theological, patristic, and biblical studies. But if the *return to the sources of the liturgy* did not have as its goal *the return to the liturgy as source*, the entire project would be useless, or of secondary importance at best. From this point of view, Parsch was *a keen theorist of the liturgical movement* because he saw, long before many others, the danger of a *ressourcement* that did not have as its primary end the rediscovery of the liturgy as *fons*.

We can almost say that the concept of liturgy will always be misunderstood where it is viewed only as

16

a concept. It is also and always an action, an activity, an event. It cannot be confined to the intellectualism of definitions; it presses toward a symbolic-ritual embodiment of the church's understanding of itself. For this reason, the relationship between concept and action stands at the heart of a systematic rethinking that, for Parsch, translates immediately into the need to bring all the baptized—not just the ordained ministers—to a full liturgical-ecclesial subjectivity.

This corresponds to that methodological and epistemological need that represents one of the most notable achievements of the twentieth-century liturgical movement, recently expressed well by Giorgio Bonaccorso: "(Liturgical) knowledge is internal to its object, with the consequence that theological reflection upon it must happen, at least in part, from within and by way of liturgical praxis: the (theological) method is internal to the liturgical object."[11]

Only when it can truly be said of our religious practice that—to use Blondel's terms—"the relationship between thought and action are at the same time preserved, completed, and overturned"[12] can we fully understand Parsch's beautiful definition of liturgy as the "formal principle" of the church: "Liturgy is the most authentic manifestation of the church's life. It is the church's face and the church's mouth. What the church feels, thinks, and does are each manifested in

[11] G. Bonaccorso, "I principali orientamenti dello studio della liturgia," in *Liturgia opus Trinitatis. Epistemologia liturgica*, ed. E. Carr, Studia Anselmiana 133, Analecta liturgica 24 (Rome: Centro Studi S. Anselmo, 2002), 95–121, here 97.

[12] M. Blondel, *L'azione. Saggio di una critica della vita e di una scienza della prassi* (Cinisello B.: Ed. Paoline, 1993), 526.

its liturgy. To be precise, it is *the formal principle* of the church."[13]

Given all of this, and in the light of what we have already considered, it is clear that Pius Parsch anticipated *Sacrosanctum Concilium*'s luminous understanding of the liturgy as *fons et culmen*. But this requires a theoretical-practical understanding of liturgy in which active participation and the universal priesthood are *not optional or peripheral elements* but *structural foundations* of the ecclesial experience of the disciples of Christ.[14] This is why the reform of the liturgy inevitably leads to the reform of the church!

Some of those who work in theology and ecclesial ministry today have forgotten Parsch's important insights. For this reason, the study of his thought,[15] though it dates from before the reform, can be a great help in rereading that reform in both its spirit and its content. More specifically, it can shed great light on the central concept of participation and our current difficulties with it.

---

[13] Parsch, *Le renouveau liturgique*, 21.

[14] Helpful considerations of the principle theological questions related to the structural significance of "active participation" are found in two recent essays: A. Cardita, "'*Actuosa participatio*': Reflexao à volta de uma noçao chave na 'questao litùrgica,'" *Humanistica e Teologia* 25 (2004): 87–104; P. De Clerck, "La participation active. Perspectives historico-liturgiques de Pie X à Vatican II," *Questions Liturgiques* 85 (2004): 11–29.

[15] For a complete bibliography on Parsch, see A. Redtenbacher, "Pius Parsch in der liturgiewissenschaftlichen Rezeption. Veröffentlichte und unveröffentlichte Arbeiten über Pius Parsch," *Heiliger Dienst* 58 (2004): 142–67.

3. ANCIENT AND MODERN "MISUNDERSTANDINGS" IN PARSCH'S APPRAISAL OF *MEDIATOR DEI* (1947)

At this point, we have to be clear about a simple fact. The liturgy cannot be understood as a "concept" alone; such an understanding is inadequate to the task of resolving the "the liturgical question." There is almost a parallelism between the condition of the first phase of the liturgical movement, of which Parsch was a part, and our current circumstances, in the so-called third phase of the movement, which began with the completion of the reform of the rites that followed Vatican II.

It was already clear in Parsch's time that the recovery of a more developed and theologically profound concept of liturgy called for liturgy to be returned to its status as *the principle, source, and inspiration of Christian life*. The task of the reform, which Parsch knew would come, was simply to make itself *the instrument by which the church could truly be formed by the liturgy*. Only those who had recognized this process as necessary and who had not neglected the "pastoral" and "popular" phase of the liturgical movement could really understand this fully at the time.[16]

On the other hand, those who were only concerned with *developing a more adequate concept of liturgy* were less prepared and ended up falling into various errors and misunderstandings. This is perhaps the most

---

[16] We can therefore repeat that *for liturgy to translate itself into "action" and "action of the people" is part of the very nature of liturgy*. This demonstrates the theoretical—and not only practical—importance of Parsch's work. Quite rightly, then, one can say that his contribution must necessarily be understood as expressing the *essential* nature of worship (and a fundamental theology of worship).

serious mistake, and the one most charged with consequence, then as now.

Even today, in fact, the way forward seems clear to some: to perfect the reform in all its aspects and to make sure that it is fully implemented, disciplinarily or normatively. This is a path that is as "reasonable" as it is "naive" and "superficial." In reality, it is clear that unless we enter into a phase of *initiation into the ecclesial life of faith that draws upon the new rites*, the reform will have been for nothing.

In the light of these brief reflections, it seems important that we pause to consider some of what has been said about Parsch's understanding of the encyclical *Mediator Dei* (1947). In an important study of Parsch's response to this encyclical, Th. Maas-Ewerd speaks of Parsch's "misunderstanding" of the document. Particularly decisive in his negative judgment is Parsch's initial reaction to *Mediator Dei*, which Parsch understood to be an "attack on his liturgical work."[17] This perception colored his entire approach to the encyclical, resulting in a pessimism that cannot be otherwise explained. As Maas-Ewert notes, the same document that Giovanni Battista Montini (later Pope Paul VI) spoke of as the "Magna Carta" of the liturgical movement was judged by Parsch to be an "invective against the liturgical movement."

In reality, I believe it is unfair to Parsch to reduce his judgment to an overly sensitive reaction to criticism.

---

[17] Th. Maas-Ewerd, "Zur Reaktion Pius Parsch auf die Enzyklika *Mediator Dei*," in *Mit sanfter Zähigkeit. Pius Parsch und die biblisch-liturgische Erneuerung*, ed. N. Höslinger and Th. Maas-Ewerd (Klosterneuburg: Oesterreichisches Katholisches Bibelwerk, 1979), 199–214, here 201.

This interpretation betrays a reading of *Mediator Dei* that, in fact, recent scholarly work as well as recent developments of the magisterium help to correct. Let us look briefly at these two levels of the question in order to note some consequences.

On the one hand, recent theological rereadings of the encyclical have made note of a more complex and nuanced relationship in the document between openness and intransigence, progress and regress, than was previously recognized.[18]

On the other hand, the incorporation of the "defensive" passages of *Mediator Dei*[19] in more recent church documents confirms a weakness in the encyclical that Parsch recognized fifty years ago: that is, the contradiction between its *openness, on an abstract level, to a renewed concept of liturgy and its closure, on a concrete*

---

[18] For a careful evaluation of the recent discussion, see the excellent contributions of A. Catella, "Dalla Costituzione conciliare *Sacrosanctum Concilium* all'enciclica *Mediator Dei*," in AA.VV., *La Mediator Dei e il Centro di Azione Liturgica: 50 anni alla luce del movimento liturgico*, Bibliotheca "Ephemerides Liturgicae," Sectio Pastoralis 18 (Rome, C.L.V.: Ed. Liturgiche, 1998), 11–43; and C. Braga, "La natura della liturgia nella *Mediator Dei* e nella *Sacrosanctum Concilium*," in *Liturgia opus Trinitatis. Epistemologia liturgica*, ed. E. Carr, Studia Anselmiana 133, Analecta liturgica 24 (Rome, Centro Studi S. Anselmo, 2002), 25–48. Useful for the reconstruction of the context is also L. Brandolini, "Il 50^ della *Mediator Dei* e del 'Cento di Azione Liturgica,'" in AA.VV., *Iniziazione cristiana degli adulti oggi*, Atti della XXVI Settimana di Studio dell'APL, Seiano di Vico Equense (NA), 31 agosto–5 settembre 1997, BELS 99 (Rome, CLV, Ed. Liturgiche, 1998), 339–54.

[19] Suffice it here to mention nn. 39–42 of the recent Instruction of the Congregation for Divine Worship and the Discipline of the Sacraments *Redemptionis Sacramentum* as an example of an objectively "regressive" approach to the notion of "participation" in *Mediator Dei*.

level, to the concept of participation and of universal priest-hood. As a result, and despite the fact that the Council did indeed draw much from it, *Mediator Dei* remains locked in the preconciliar past.

We might therefore ask, concluding this third point: Who is really the one who misunderstood the encyclical? What is the real "misunderstanding"? We must recognize that it was Parsch's concept of liturgy (which was broader than the more intellectualized thinking of others of his time, not unlike that of many today) that allowed him to recognize the limits of *Mediator Dei* in ways that others missed. Let us explore this "gap" a bit more thoroughly now by briefly comparing the perspectives of *Mediator Dei* and *Sacrosanctum Concilium*.

4. *MEDIATOR DEI* AND *SACROSANCTUM CONCILIUM*: TWO DIFFERENT UNDERSTANDINGS OF PARTICIPATION IN THE LITURGY

For many centuries the theological-ecclesial approach to the liturgy—and specifically to the Eucharist—was completely preoccupied with confessional polemics. Catholic anti-Protestantism and Protestant anti-Catholicism reduced the position of both sides to a matter of valiant opposition to a dangerous enemy.

The echo of this situation is still heard in *Mediator Dei* (see nn. 66–137, on worship of the Eucharist),[20]

---

[20] [The numbering of the sections of *Mediator Dei* noted here and in the following paragraphs follows the English version of the encyclical available on the Vatican web site. This numbering differs from that offered in the original Italian version of *Beyond Pius V*, since the author referred to a translation of the encyclical published by Edizioni San Paolo in 1997, which numbered the sections differently. (The official Latin editio typica of the encyclical does not include numbering of the sections.) —Trans.]

despite the fact that by 1947, the fruits of the liturgical movement had nearly reached maturity and begun to transform the climate previously marked only by apologetics.[21] Nevertheless, *Mediator Dei* addressed three fundamental topics related to the Eucharist:

a. the nature of the eucharistic sacrifice (nn. 66–79)
b. participation of the faithful in the eucharistic sacrifice (nn. 80–111)
c. eucharistic communion (nn. 112–28)

Following these, the document considers the topic of eucharistic adoration (nn. 129–37).

The encyclical approaches each of these three topics with great reserve, careful distinctions, and strong prohibitions. Its most relevant points are as follows:

a.) The sacrificial nature of Eucharist is reaffirmed and defined in great detail, according to the teaching of the Council of Trent. New perspectives are suggested, drawing strongly on the encyclical *Mystici Corporis*, a long citation of which closes the section.

b.) Participation of the faithful is understood as being "united as closely as possible" with Christ, but it hastens to exclude any suggestion of equality between laity and clergy and rejects criticism of "masses which are offered privately." It advises a sort of "devotional parallelism" (for the people) alongside the eucharistic rite.[22]

---

[21] Cf. Catella, *Da Sacrosanctum Concilium*, passim.

[22] It is interesting to note that the concept of the *participation of the faithful* in *Mediator Dei* is essentially related not to the *rite* but to one's *state of mind* (cf. n. 81). And so those who have difficulty understanding the liturgical rites or who do not feel like participating in

c.) Regarding Communion, the first point made is the fact that the integrity of the sacrifice is not compromised when only the priest communicates. A famous expression from the *Imitatio Christi*—"Remain on in secret and take delight in your God" (see n. 126)—summarizes the model of "participation" proposed by *Mediator Dei*. We can see here the effect of the division, even in temporal terms, of the Eucharist into "assisting at Mass" and "receiving Communion." This is, broadly outlined and extremely synthesized, where the matter stood when the new perspective of *Sacrosanctum Concilium* burst forth a generation later.

The new perspective introduced by *Sacrosanctum Concilium* decisively shifts the priorities of the church's approach to the Eucharist.[23] The most significant ele-

---

the eucharistic sacrifice "can adopt some other method which proves easier for certain people; for instance, they can lovingly meditate on the mysteries of Jesus Christ or perform other exercises of piety or recite prayers which, though they differ from the sacred rites, are still essentially in harmony with them" (n. 108). This explicit counsel of *participative parallelism* does not foresee the novelty that *Sacrosanctum Concilium* would introduce, making *ritual form* and *active participation* inseparable. It is precisely this difference that the Council sought to recover and authoritatively propose.

[23] Chapter 2, titled *De sacrosancto eucharistiae mysteri*, includes eleven numbered sections dedicated to the Eucharist, organized in this way:

- 47: the Mass and the paschal mystery
- 48–49: active participation of the faithful
- 50: the reform of the *Ordo missae*
- 51: an opening up of the riches of Scripture
- 52: the homily

ment is the rediscovery and reconsideration of the close interrelationship between three different levels of discourse and experience that had previously been kept separate and juxtaposed:

a.) the *"narrative" definition of Eucharist*
b.) the essential nature of *active participation* of the faithful
c.) the *specific form* of such participation

I would venture to say that this final point offers the greatest differences with respect to past thinking—and in some ways to thinking today! Article 48, on active participation of the faithful, teaches that the faithful should take part *"per ritus et preces id [=eucharisticum mysterium] bene intelligentes."*[24] Here we find official recognition of *the inadequacy of the participation only "in one's mind"* that had previously been promoted by the liturgical movement and the reform it spurred.

It is clear, then, that the true motive of the reform consists in the possibility of *understanding* the eucharistic mystery *per ritus et preces*, that is, in the conscious, prayerful, and active participation in the *liturgical action*. The *action*, then, is the primary means by which one understands the liturgy. Of primary

---

– 53: the prayer of the faithful
– 54: the vernacular language
– 55: Communion *sub utraque* ["under both kinds" —Trans.]
– 56: the unity of the Mass
– 57: concelebration

Even this list of topics is enough to highlight the profoundly different point of view with which the Eucharist is now regarded.

[24] [The English version of the document reads: "through a good understanding of the rites and prayers." —Trans.]

consideration, in this view, is not *the meaning in the mind* (*actus animae*) but rather the sign and the corporate act (*usus rerum exteriorum*) that express the meaning. The reform of the eucharistic rite is therefore motivated essentially by the need *to recover, fully and for all*, this ritual-prayer level of *eucharistic understanding*. In other words, we are talking about not a reform aimed solely at a better intellectual understanding but a change of perspective and an experiential recovery in view of a new and fundamental way of understanding the truth of the Eucharist, in balance between sensibility and intellect. It is the *rituum forma* (SC 49), the ritual form, that assures the full pastoral efficacy of the eucharistic sacrifice.[25]

This perspective also changes—almost inevitably—the general tone with which many other liturgical questions are approached. Understanding questions in terms of the *actio sacris* means being concerned first of all with recovering the fullness of ritual gesture rather than the integrality of the meaning.[26] The consideration of the fullness of the participation concentrates the attention on the *act* rather than on the *meaning*, and that also modifies profoundly the method of eucharistic theology. The "positive" takes precedence over the "negative," the "propositive" over the "de-

---

[25] For an explanation of the theme of "ritual form," see Loris Della Pietra, *Rituum forma e teologia dei sacramenti. La nozione di forma dopo la Ri-forma liturgica del Concilio Vaticano II* (Padova: EMP-Abbazia S. Giustina, 2012).

[26] Here the liturgical-sacramental approach clearly prevails over the dogmatic-disciplinary and/or subjective-spiritual approach. The logic of "minimum necessary" is replaced by that of "greatest possible."

fensive," what is articulated over what is essential; in other words, *with this new mentality introduced by the Council—but long prepared for by the liturgical move-ment—the accident is not irrelevant to the substance.* We might say that in the Eucharist, thanks to these new considerations, one rediscovers that the accidents are not accidental.

This, as we have said, modifies the theology and the practice of the Eucharist, because it moves us beyond the logic of what part of the ritual is minimally neces-sary and sufficient for the mind of the participant. On the contrary, in this new perspective, such an approach is not only no longer enough but even misleading and the source of serious misunderstandings.

In this perspective, the real and most serious li-turgical abuse is the reduction of the Eucharist to its minimum, to its essentials, to its conceptual skeleton. It is a perspective that gives rise to an urgent need for a full *spacio-temporal understanding of the eucharistic action*, recovering all the richness of the readings from Scrip-ture, the homily, the prayer of the faithful, a language that is understood, Communion with bread and wine, unity of the celebration, and possibility of concele-bration. It must be noted: not one of these elements is traditionally understood to be *ad necessitatem*, but all of them are *ad solemnitatem*. In the old perspective, they are all dispensable elements. With respect to *the theo-logical meaning* of the Eucharist, they were considered to be contingent, accessory, accidental. When the litur-gical action—and not only its meaning—is placed at the center of our conception of the Eucharist, each of its "parts" is *a symbolic-ritual act that theologically qualifies the Eucharist*. The real impact that this change of priorities brings with it, both on the level of pastoral-existential experience and on the level of theological-conceptual reflection, is not yet fully appreciated. While Pius Parsch's authoritative teaching took account of and, in its own way, largely anticipated this vision, such is not the case in our time, when it is not difficult to point to instances of real regression.

5. A TROUBLING CONFIRMATION: THE RECENT INSTRUCTION *REDEMPTIONIS SACRAMENTUM*

The tendency identified above is strongly confirmed in the instruction *Redemptionis Sacramentum*,[27] the title of which comes, not insignificantly, from the *Oratio super oblata* of the votive Mass *de Dei misericordia*. Leaving aside for the moment consideration of the document's tone, I limit myself here to exploring its approach to the idea of "participation" in the Eucharist.

It is true that *Redemptionis Sacramentum* notes explicitly that it has no intention of being exhaustive in approach: it "does not intend to express the entirety of the Christian vision of the eucharist" (RS 8). Despite this clear affirmation, the text does not shrink from offering criteria for a comprehensive rereading of the eucharistic celebration, one that inevitably gives rise to a certain tension with the conciliar tradition of Vatican II. It is important to point out that the Council's teaching on the Eucharist includes important points that *Redemptionis Sacramentum* fails to mention. Furthermore, where the teaching of *Sacrosanctum Concilium* and *Redemptionis*

---

[27] [Issued by the Congregation for Divine Worship and the Discipline of the Sacraments, with the subtitle "On certain matters to be observed or to be avoided regarding the Most Holy Eucharist," on March 25, 2004. —Trans.]

Sacramentum overlap, that of *Redemptionis Sacramentum* is offered in very different language and with a very different point of view. The document seems barely aware of this, and *it tries to do two things: while limiting itself to reaffirming norms already in force*, it proposes an objectively "regressive" rereading of eucharistic participation, *more in line with* Mediator Dei *than with* Sacrosanctum Concilium.

Chapter 2 in particular ("The Participation of the Lay Christian Faithful in the Eucharistic Celebration") manifests most strongly the tensions between the document's disciplinary norms and the pastoral and theological convictions of the Second Vatican Council.

First of all, despite references to conciliar teaching (which seem merely rhetorical in nature), the chapter reveals an ecclesiology marked by profound clericalism, that is, by a deep divide between clerics and lay faithful, which is founded in an understanding of the Eucharist that is strongly and substantially sacrificial, while only minimally and peripherally communal (see RS 37–38). What results is an understanding of active participation of the people of God in the eucharistic celebration that better reflects the reductive and still substantially Tridentine reading of *Mediator Dei* than the teaching of Vatican II (cf. RS 39–42).

In this reading, the participation of the laity in the Eucharist is something essentially different from the celebration of the ordained minister. The message conveyed indirectly is that the laity participate in the Eucharist (but they do not celebtrate it and therefore are not priests), while the ordained ministers celebrate the Eucharist and as such can be called priests (as the document does from the first page to the last). *Redemptionis Sacramentum* 41, for example, explicitly proposes the parallelism between different forms of participation as model for understanding the participation of the laity (borrowing it explicitly from *Mediator Dei*). The following number (RS 42) rereads the conciliar tradition of "celebrating assembly" tendentiously, as an "abuse," not in the context of its great ecclesiological, spiritual, and existential richness, but merely on the level of the distinction between clergy and laity at Mass, offering only caution in the use of the expression.

More generally, we can note that the document draws unfortunately from theoretical errors found in more recent liturgical theology, in which one sometimes finds understandings of "active participation" that have little to do with the church's conciliar and postconciliar journey. They offer a contrapositioning between "interior" and "exterior" participation that harkens back to medieval efforts to identify the "minimum necessary" that must be rejected today. The result is that the fundamental motives that led, with great effort, to the reform are forgotten and the justifications for it are undermined, making way for revisionism and a temptation to "reform the reform."

This is the horizon of the sacramental and ecclesial rethinking that has produced the current decline of the concept of "participated liturgy." What is necessary now is for the form of liturgical participation to be understood again as ritual in nature, for the matter to be redefined first of all as historical-symbolic, and for the minister to be seen again as fundamentally plural, articulated, and communitarian in structure. Only then will liturgy be—truly and not just rhetorically—the *culmen et fons* of the life of the church.

But to ask such questions today about the genealogical power of the liturgy for the church—an *ecclesia* that truly lives *de eucharistia*—means casting a glance in this tangle of relationships toward different experiences of the liturgy. And it must be done, I am convinced, with intentions that are anything but iconoclastic or antitraditional; rather, it must be done with a true passion for the equilibrium of the tradition, an equilibrium that has become disturbed by those who invent objective-disciplinary reasons and/or devotionalistic-spiritual reasons over against the authentic liturgical-sacramental reasons. This is the aim of the third phase, the "realistic" phase, of the liturgical movement mentioned by Guardini in 1953 (and cited in the epigraph of this chapter) that today calls the church to approach active participation as a matter of the initiation of Christians into their rightful place in the church, always as subjects (of rights) and objects (of duties) but, most important, as witness-symbols (of gifts), that is, of an ecclesial identity marked—in body, in heart, and in mind—by the gracious and merciful lordship of Jesus, crucified and risen over the mysterious and always tormented history of humanity and of the world.

Chapter 3

Before and After *Sacrosanctum Concilium*: The Relevance of the Liturgical Movement

> The hour has come, it seems to us, in which the truth about the Church of Christ must be explored, ordered, and expressed, perhaps not with those solemn statements that are dogmatic definitions, but with declarations by which the Church, with more explicit and authoritative teaching, declares what it thinks about itself.
>
> —Pope Paul VI
> Opening of the Second Session
> of the Second Vatican Council
> September 29, 1963

In this chapter, I would like to explore several questions raised by the occasion of the fiftieth anniversary of *Sacrosanctum Concilium*. This anniverary offers an important moment for reflection and assessment. One important distinction should be made from the start. It is one thing to speak of the fiftieth anniversary of *Sacrosanctum Concilium*; it is another thing to speak of fifty years of the liturgical reform; it is still another thing to look to *Sacrosanctum Concilium* as the beginning of something or as the end of something else.

The argument I wish to present here is that *a change of perspective is necessary within the church today, a dif-*

ferent point of view, in order to promote and protect the authentic intentions of Sacrosanctum Concilium. If we limit ourselves to considering *Sacrosanctum Concilium* solely as a beginning point, we already have run off the rails and jeopardized an authentic interpretation of the document.

We must try to understand the relationship between *Sacrosanctum Concilium* and the liturgical reform within a wider time span, that is, in the context of the dynamic between the initial emergence of a "liturgical question" and attempts by the liturgical movement to offer a response to it. Today we can, with some embarrassment, come to terms with and resolve the struggle between the defenders of the reform and those who would dig its grave only if we can manage this broader understanding. That is to say: we can understand the last fifty years only by looking to the fifty years that preceded them and to the century as a whole. Ironically, grasping *the fifty years after Sacrosanctum Concilium* is only possible by rediscovering *the fifty years before it!* This is the hypothesis we will explore in the pages ahead. I want to make it clear from the start, laying my cards on the table.

We have to admit that this change in our understanding of the liturgical movement represents one of the most precious fruits of the liturgical reform, and yet it demands that we reconsider how we think of the reform of the rites that was such a prominent aspect of the broader reform.

The *liturgical question* lies at the foundation of our ecclesial thinking and living today, with various impacts at the christological, ecclesiological, historical, political, and ecumenical levels. But there is no doubt that our understanding of the liturgical movement is changing, from being simply *the preparation and premise of the reform* to being *the context and interpreter of it*. The liturgical movement can no longer be understood simply as the prologue and premise of the official revision of the texts and gestures. Rather, it is the context that gives meaning to the reform and that guides its reception.[1]

In reality, it is impossible to understand the phenomenon of the liturgical movement apart from the particular cultural climate of late modernity in Europe (following the French Revolution), from which sprang a new interest in Christian liturgy. This new intuition was at the same time practical and theoretical and, I repeat, is fully explained only as response to the challenge of late modernity. In our own "postmodern" times, it takes on a new light and a new challenge.

The late modern age approached the "liturgical question" on two levels: that of an *initiation into the rite*[2] and *the reform of the rites themselves*. Although it is clear today that the latter approach ultimately took precedence over the former, it never really succeeded in bringing about the *aggiornamento* that was hoped for. This is the fault not—as often is mistakenly suggested—of the reform of the rites as such but of the context in which they were introduced. By itself, we must confess and admit today, fifty years after the

---

[1] It is therefore evident that my hypothesis understands the "liturgical movement" as a phenomenon that *includes* the Council, not one that *concludes with* the Council. This calls for a complex historiographical revision, which demands courage to be undertaken. This revision is necessary today in light of problems that cannot be accounted for by the "classical" historiography.

[2] [That is, the formation of the Christian people to a deeper and more authentic understanding of the rites and what they call for in Christian living. —Trans.]

promulgation of *Sacrosanctum Concilium*, that *the way the liturgical reform was prepared for was quite different from the way it was implemented*. This difference between preparation and implementation—between the careful development of a broad awareness of the need to confront the *liturgical question* at the two levels noted above and the conscious commitment to carry out a reform of the rites as an important (though never exclusive) aspect of a response to that question—seems to me to be the most relevant element in truly understanding what happened in the story of the twentieth-century liturgical movement.[3]

Thus, I believe that restoring the *relevance* of the liturgical reform in our day depends on the precious rediscovery of the *aspects of it that are considered outdated, dull, and not really translated into clear and distinct ideas*. The reform will succeed by looking less like a reform as we have known it. Indeed, it is this *nonintellectualistic (but still intelligent and sensible!) aspect* of the reform that gives it its real meaning today and enables it to respond adequately to the liturgical question, and this is the aspect I wish to consider briefly here. In fact, it is only by returning to *this "outdated" aspect of the reform that we can ever hope for the liturgical movement to be relevant* and effective, to represent a movement of the Spirit among us and not just something to get coverage in newspapers.[4]

---

[3] Cf. A. Grillo, *La nascita della liturgia nel XX secolo. Saggio sul rapporto tra Movimento Liturgico e (post-)Modernità* (Assisi: Cittadella, 2003).

[4] The liturgical movement is essentially *antiliberal*, but that does not mean that it is necessarily *antimodern*. Indeed, its profound criticisms of the "liberal" (that is, individualistic, rationalistic, and

In this chapter, I propose a series of "forgotten truths" about the liturgical movement, convinced that the movement's relevance depends on the rediscovery of what might be considered most outdated about it. We shall briefly consider five points: first, the theological method of the liturgical movement; second, the two anthropological shifts of the twentieth century; third, a proposal for a new understanding of the historical development of the liturgical movement; and finally, the two meanings of *ressourcement* and the liturgical reform. Following these, I offer seven concluding theses and five examples of current issues that these ideas might help us address better.

1. THE THEOLOGICAL METHOD OF THE LITURGICAL MOVEMENT

In an effort to leave behind a dried up (systematic) rationalism without falling into a dried up (historical) positivism, the early liturgical movement introduced a *new theological method*. Indeed, the introduction of

---

intellectualistic) presuppositions that are shared by modernity and theology give it a particularly "modern" (and perhaps even postmodern) character. Here, I think, lies one of the unresolved questions of our implementation and rethinking of the liturgical question: we continue to think about (and to practice) the experience of liturgy from an *essentially liberal perspective* (that is, based on the political principle of a personal freedom that is untouched by any externality) *but with a fundamentally antimodern attitude* (rejecting the value of modernity), while I believe that, in the prevalent spirit of the liturgical movement, we must deepen the awareness among Christians of the *nonliberal nature of the ecclesial perspective* (that is, an experience of the world, of God, and of self that begins not from a freedom that is already mine but from the gift of freedom) but do it in profound dialogue with modernity and postmodernity.

this method proved useful to both systematic and historical theology. It was necessary because the theological method that had marked the work of scholars such as Maurice Festugière, Odo Casel, and Romano Guardini—characterized respectively by the recovery of "liturgical realism," "global thinking," and "polar opposition," and which overcame the opposition between theology and anthropology in the ways they understood the *act of liturgy*—had been forgotten.

We can identify *three phases* of the liturgical movement, and with each successive phase the truth of this new theological method was progressively forgotten, until it almost disappeared. This, curiously, had a significant impact on the relationship between the liturgical movement and the liturgical reform. In fact, the conception of the liturgical movement as *preparation* of the reform seems almost to confirm the idea—simplistic and naive—that the answer to the liturgical question is found only in a reform prepared for by the recovery of the ancient sources.

What is clear today, however, is that the reform of the rites was only an intermediate step along the way of liturgical renewal, which—with the reform complete—must now recover the most authentic aspects of its identity. We can say that the liturgical movement has a role not only *before* the reform but also and above all *after* it, so that it may continue with the business of *forming Christians in the reformed rites and by means of them*. This is not a purpose extrinsic to the movement's identity but part of its very nature.

This becomes clear only when we can consider the theological methodology of the liturgical movement in new categories. In particular, this means leaving behind the common contrapositions between systematic knowledge and historical knowledge or between the theological shift and the anthropological shift. Regarding the former, we must acknowledge that the very first issue of the *Jahrbuch für Liturgiewissenschaft* (1921) included a heated discussion on method in liturgical studies. And yet, none of the great figures of the first generation of liturgical studies were solely systematicians or solely historians; rather, they also used the new human sciences to help understand the ritual underpinnings of the act of faith and of theological knowledge.

On the other hand, attentiveness to theological method by liturgical studies is as old as the liturgical movement itself. In fact, while it is certainly true that the liturgical movement is a complex phenomenon that includes many dimensions (ecclesial, institutional, religious, political, spiritual, etc.),[5] it remains impossible to grasp its true nature without recognizing it as being fundamentally *the rediscovery of the theological nature of liturgy*.[6] The liturgical movement arose pri-

---

[5] A lucid introduction to this plurality of aspects is offered succinctly by F. Brovelli, "Radici, acquisizioni, istanze del Movimento Liturgico nel nostro secolo," in AA.VV., *Assisi 1956–1986: il Movimento liturgico tra riforma conciliare e attese del popolo di Dio* (Assisi, Cittadella, 1987), 47–74.

[6] Cf. R. Messner, "Was ist systematische Liturgiewissenschaft? Ein Entwurf in sieben Thesen," *Archiv für Liturgiewissenschaft* 40 (1998): 257–74. The author makes clear from the start that „die Forderung einer systematisch-theologischen Erforschung der Liturgie als notwendige Ergänzung der Liturgiegeschichtsforschung *gehört zu den Konstitutionsbedingungen der Liturgiewissenschaft als eines eigenständigen theologischen Fachs"* (257, italics mine). The author also points out that this need is ancient but still largely unrealized by liturgical studies.

marily *as a response to the "liturgical question," that is, as a careful exploration of the "crisis" of the relationship between "secularized" modernity and the ritual experience of faith and an attempt to offer a theoretical and practical answer to this bewildering new ecclesial reality.* Having said that, we should also point out that the vital interest of the liturgical movement also necessarily includes the interest of research: in a certain sense it is true of both historical and theological research that one can seek only that which has in some way already been found.[7]

This assumption, however, is rarely acknowledged today; on the contrary, it is almost presumed that one studies anything but this. Such errors are not unique to "secular"—that is, nontheological, or even antitheological—studies. It also applies to more strictly theological studies, and it even represents a consensus within liturgical studies. In fact, while "secular" studies tend not to perceive the theological depth of the question

---

[7] This means, in more explicit terms, that we can find in the liturgical movement a specific theological interest only when we take great care not to absolutize "our" interests as readers/scholars. If, for example, we insist on starting from the principle—considered "obvious"—that faith as "conversion" always precedes its liturgical and cultic expression, then it becomes highly unlikely that we will be able to grasp what is most original about what the liturgical movement has said and still has to say to us. This *hermeneutic condition* will be precisely the place where historical method and theological method in theological studies encounter one another. The relationship between the "disinterested," "value-free" knowledge of historical studies and the "non-indifferent" experience of ritual worship calls into question the self-understanding of theology as much as it does history; on the topic of the modern relevance of "the believing conscience," cf. P. Sequeri, "La qualità spirituale del post-moderno," in P. Sequeri, *Sensibili allo Spirito. Umanesimo religioso e ordine degli affetti* (Milan: Glossa, 2001), 3–44.

of the relationship between faith and secularization—quickly reducing the issue to concepts of a hegemonic project or a nostalgia for medieval Christianity[8]—theological studies tend instead to consider it "obvious" that the liturgical movement is simply a precursor and premise to the event that was the Council and in particular to the liturgical reform, which is perceived as the "solution" to the problem. This thinking, however, risks introducing two grave errors.

First, it fails to account for the historical complexity of the "liturgical question" as a theological problem of modernity, never encountered by classical theology. The identification of concern for the liturgy with a restorationist officialdom or with an intransigent reaction to modernity can be maintained only by oversimplifying not only the historical data but also the true motivations that gave rise to many of the liturgical debates and discussions of the twentieth century. On one hand, we still find the classic perception of the liturgical

[8] The most interesting example of this approach to our theme is the well-documented work of M. Pajano, *Liturgia e società nel novecento. Percorsi del movimento liturgico di fronte ai processi di secolarizzazione*, Biblioteca di storia sociale 28 (Rome: Edizioni di Storia e Letteratura, 2000). A "political" reading of the liturgical movement, while including undoubtedly relevant aspects, does not, however, seem to grasp its "whole" and carries out a systematic reduction of the movement's most authentic intentions to phenomenon of a different kind. An exemplary case of the strengths and the limits of this approach is also found in Daniele Menozzi's essay included in the same volume; Menozzi's research depends explicitly on Pajano's important work. An excellent work of an entirely different nature, concerned above all to "save" the medieval period from its liturgical incomprehension, is A. Angenendt, *Liturgik und Historik. Gab es eine organische Liturgie-Entwicklung?*, Quaestiones Disputatae 189 (Freiburg-Basel-Wien, 2001).

movement as a dangerous phenomenon, rooted in Enlightenment-style reasoning and its intellectualization of faith.[9] On the other, reducing it to intransigence reveals an understanding of it that is incomplete, if not a caricaturization of it. At the center, I think, must instead be placed the complex relationship (which is not only one of "power") between the conscience of the believer and the modern world, within which the rediscovery of "celebrated faith" has made possible "a Catholic modernity."[10]

Second, what results from this oversimplification is the banalization of the Second Vatican Council and the liturgical reform that resulted from it, reducing both

---

[9] One of the first global understandings of this kind is found in W. Trapp, *Vorgeschichte und Ursprung der liturgischen Bewegung, vorwiegend in Hinsicht auf das deutsche Sprachgebiet* (Regensburg: Pustet, 1940). In addition to this, we cannot fail to note, with appropriate nuances, H. U. von Balthasar (*Solo l'amore è credibile* [Rome: Borla, 1991], 46n15), J.-L. Marion (cf. especially the two "eucharistic" essays "Del sito eucaristico della teologia" and "Il presente e il dono," in J.-L. Marion, *Dio senza essere* [Milan, Jaca Book, 1984; (ET: "Of the Eucharistic Site of Theology" and "The Present and the Gift," in J.-L. Marion, *God without Being*, trans. Thomas A. Carlson, 2nd ed. [Chicago: University of Chicago Press, 2012], 139–60 and 161–82, respectively. —Trans.)]); and also J. Ratzinger (*Introduzione allo spirito della liturgia* [Cinisello B.: San Paolo, 2001; (ET: J. Ratzinger, *The Spirit of the Liturgy* [San Francisco: Ignatius, 2000] —Trans.)]). For an interesting assessment of the contemporary debate, cf. K. Irwin, "Critiquing Recent Liturgical Critics," *Worship* 74 (2000): 2–19.

[10] It would be useful for theology and liturgical history to acquire the lucid balance that Charles Taylor demonstrates in his essay "Una modernità cattolica?," *Annali di Studi religiosi* 1 (2001): 405–27, where he confronts admirably all the complex questions of the relationship between secularization and belief.

of these great ecclesial phenomena to the realization of ideas conceived too unilaterally and inadequately, due to a shortsighted vision, often without awareness of the constitutive encounter that the liturgical movement initiated not only with the church's own life and history but also with the external culture and with late modernity's new sense of the human person. As the liturgical reform was carried out, everything about the liturgical question that called for theological research and reflection—not only a drawing from the past its own authenticity, but also the rediscovery in the liturgical celebration of the paschal mystery as an irreducible "source" of its own identity[11]—was quickly hidden away.

2. THE TWO ANTHROPOLOGICAL SHIFTS OF THE TWENTIETH CENTURY
Twentieth-century theology is marked by what has been called an "anthropological shift," a great reconciliation between theology and anthropology, between the church and modernity. With the autonomous growth of anthropology in the nineteenth century, a strong opposition between the two fields had developed, so much so that theology, in order to safeguard its own conceptions of reality, found itself compelled to dismiss and condemn the concurrent anthropological interpretations.

[11] On the question of "source" as a fundamental issue of the liturgical movement, and also as a key inspiration of the yearning for *ressourcement* that marked the liturgical rebirth of the twentieth century, see A. Grillo, "Liturgia come 'fons' e iniziazione alla fede: una (ri)scoperta nel suo percorso storico e nei suoi nodi teorici," *Quaderni della Segreteria Generale CEI* 5, no. 7 (2001): 54–67.

With the anthropological shift, it appeared that a new equilibrium had been found and that the preconceived condemnations between the two fields had been left behind. This reconciliation between *faith* and *reason* brought a rehabilitation—in various ways—of a place in Christian tradition for all that is subjective, interior, free, transcendental, individual, experiential, symbolic, and "anonymous." All these terms—which previously had sounded like synonyms for betraying the faith, the decline of the church, errors in orthodoxy, and "modernism"—became vital expressions of authentic Christian living.

We must say, however, that here liturgical-sacramental studies holds for us an interesting surprise. We can identify, in the second and third decades of the twentieth century, a "second anthropological shift." This shift—similar to the "first," but different in source and priority—also recovered the *anthropological* meaning of faith, but it did so by rediscovering the role of exteriority, community, otherness, over against the authority of interiority, individuality, identity, and freedom. It too was preoccupied with a connection between faith and reason, but it inverted the priorities and changed the sources: it proceeds from exterior to interior, and rather than being based on a metaphysical tradition, it was oriented by the new human, religious, and phenomenological sciences.[12]

---

[12] For this reason, I believe that speaking of a dialectic between the "first" and "second" anthropological shift is preferable to a contraposition between "anthropological shift" and "theological shift" (posed, for example, by M. Kunzler, "La liturgia all'inizio del terzo millennio," in *Il Concilio Vaticano II. Recezione e attualità alla luce del giubileo*, ed. R. Fisichella [Rome: San Paolo, 2000], 217–31)

In this we see the beginnings of a phenomenon that, starting in the 1980s, also marked other areas of post-conciliar theology, that is, the overcoming of the intellectualistic residue that had accumulated too much in both classical theology and the theology of the first anthropological shift. Turning away from this fundamental intellectualism, liturgical theology developed a strong interest in "phenomenological," "global," "primitive" dynamics, which assume a concept of the human person that is not primarily one of either intellect or will but as *ratio et manus, sensus et tactus*, a symbolic and ritual animal.

Here we discover that it is precisely the research undertaken by scholars of the liturgy that brought to light the limits of an anthropological shift that assumed a model of the (believing and Christian) person that was still too dependent on intellectualist concepts of the transcendental and idealistic tradition. The "second anthropological shift," on the other hand, takes seriously the challenge of the "linguistic shift" and phenomenology's orientation toward "the things themselves," using these hypotheses for "rereading" the experience of faith from the standpoint of the liturgical celebration.[13]

-----

that risks disregarding this fundamental intention of the liturgical movement. My approach, in fact, offers the dual benefit of more easily recognizing not only that *both shifts are theological but that both are radically attentive to anthropology*. The other approach would tend to see Rahner as "simply" an anthropologist and Casel as a "theologian." But this, obviously, not only fails to do justice to the two theologians but also fails to recognize the anthropological question that occupied twentieth-century theology and the liturgical movement in particular.

[13] It could go without saying that the work of Gh. Lafont and L.-M. Chauvet in France and A. N. Terrin and G. Bonaccorso in

It is interesting to note that the fascinating question of the relationship between *late modern liturgical studies*—which for the first time recognized a theological status for the action of the liturgy—and the anthropological shift in twentieth-century theology holds many surprises. The relationship between the two was gravely misunderstood in at least two different ways.

First, the predominant antimodernist bias demanded that liturgical studies had to be either radically (and providentially) opposed to or substantially (and problematically) in harmony with twentieth-century theology's anthropological shift. The long debate on the *method*, the *object*, and even the *legitimacy* of liturgical studies lasted throughout the first half of the twentieth century. Historical reconstruction today allows for a different understanding of the liturgical movement and of its ideological orientation. It appears at times as an almost Enlightenment-style rationalization of authentic tradition, and therefore supportive of the "anthropological shift"; at other times, however, it appears to be a return to eighteenth-century intransigence and antimodern reaction and therefore a rejection of the spirit and intentions of the anthropological shift.

Second, the same anthropological shift, while evaluated in a variety of ways, was almost never considered in its "liturgical component." It was understood instead as *an a-liturgical and extra-liturgical phenomenon* that only secondarily influenced the work of the first- and second-generation liturgical scholars. On the contrary, it is interesting for us to note that the liturgical movement

---

Italy are efforts, albeit with different styles, to integrate the "linguistic" and the "phenomenological shift" in the liturgical sensibility of the liturgical movement.

was born in the context of a quite fundamental anthropological interest, which became a part of the official theological discourse only much later and which can be accurately understood in terms of "another" or a "second" anthropological shift, alongside the first, but with its own important differences and peculiarities.

In a certain sense, these terminological and historical points are intended to highlight a fact of great importance but too often disregarded and obscured: that is, that *the theological work of the liturgical scholars*—by reason of the particularity of the object of their study— was by necessity done with reference to anthropological concerns, according to a particular style and method that was common at that time to other fields of theology. Most historical accounts today, for obvious reasons, choose *to divide the liturgical movement into stages within the context of a single anthropological shift.* For my part, I prefer to proceed in the opposite way: *understanding the liturgical movement and the reform of the liturgy to which it gave rise as a singular development, I divide the anthropological shift into two levels, taking place at two moments and in two styles—the "first" and the "second."*

In other words, while it is common to divide the liturgical movement into two parts, safeguarding a unitary understanding of the anthropological shift, I would like to differentiate the anthropological shift in order to recover a unitary vision—as I have described—of the liturgical movement.

This hermeneutical operation seems to me not only to be plausible but also to offer a real advantage both to historical research and to current theological studies, which are often conditioned not by objective *judgments* but by *prejudices* that exert more of an influence on the research than they are studied by it. We can list here at least four of these advantages:

a. This account permits a more faithful reading of the phenomenon of liturgy (of the ritual "data" in all its complexity and richness), eliminating or at least limiting every form of "ideologization" of the Christian rite, of reduction of the forms to contents or of contents to formalisms.

b. It allows us to recover the full depth of the liturgical movement, leaving behind the stereotype that sees it simply as "preparation" for the Council; avoiding a projection into the past of understandings that only developed later, this method recovers the fundamental freshness of the first attempts at a response to the liturgical question.

c. It allows for a different and more comprehensive understanding of all the recent problems and controversies related to the reception of the liturgical reform in ordinary Christian life and therefore for a more accurate interpretation of the different forms of "flight" (either nostaligic or relativistic) from the liturgical question that have resulted in our losing sight of the fundamental concerns of the great liturgical scholars at the beginning of the twentieth century.

d. Finally, it brings to light in a clearer and more explicit way the internal structure of the anthropological shift, making note of some aspects of it that might be less evident or even forgotten. The result of a distinction between "first" and "second" shift would therefore be important not only for a good understanding of the liturgical movement and ritual in the church today but also for an accurate grasp of the theological journey of the twentieth century.

3. A DIFFERENT ACCOUNT OF THE DEVELOPMENT OF THE LITURGICAL MOVEMENT

Every historical account not only looks to the past but also says something about the present and even to the future. It is rooted unavoidably in a particular point of observation, a present with an eye on the future. Our own account offered here, therefore, surely says as much about the first decades of the twenty-first century as it does about the beginning or the middle of the twentieth! Despite this, and even because of it, we cannot fail to offer it. Indeed, precisely in proposing this account of the historical development of the liturgical movement, I am proposing, unavoidably, a reconsidering of its meaning and its interpretation.

It is true, in fact, that much ecclesiastical historiography of the liturgical movement is still marked too deeply by *apologetic intentions*. Maria Pajano is correct when she says, with regard to the liturgical movement, that "contemporary religious historiography has up to now focused above all on its theological elaborations—mostly with an apologetic approach—neglecting . . . to place them more generally within the developing relationship between the church and society in the last century."[14]

But this defect in the historiography of the liturgical movement is not only a result of a forgetfulness of the radical opposition between liturgy and the modern spirit that was surely one of the primary interests of the early liturgical movement. Rather, it stems also

---

[14] Pajano, *Liturgia e società*, 5.

from a progressive incomprehension of the radical and profound ideas that pervaded the Christian church throughout the first half of the twentieth century and that led to the Second Vatican Council. This ignorance of the most fundamental origins of the Council, however, is found in both ecclesiastical and secular historiography. The latter, while having taken account of the important background of ecclesiastical politics and the relationship between the church and modernity and thus offering a real contribution to our understanding of the liturgical movement, has not yet grasped the decisive reason that made the liturgical movement a force, not simply for restoration, but for effective reform of the church.[15]

The idea that the liturgical movement is characterized essentially as a project in which the liturgy is understood as a "tool wielded to help bring about the return to a Christian society," while certainly a relevant component of recent events, does not seem in reality to take full account of the center of its identity, precisely because it fails to recognize in some way *liturgy's role as* fons *of Christian experience.*

This is not so much a question of a kind of "political use of the liturgy" or its functionalization in some new or old hegemonic plan so much as its irreducibility to an exercise of *an act of one who already has faith.*[16] Even if

---

[15] Interesting in this regard is A. Schilson, "Rinnovamento dallo spirito della restaurazione," *Cristianesimo nella Storia* 12 (1991): 569–602.

[16] Pajano writes that the change in understanding of the liturgical action that followed World War II was in favor of a "liturgical theology that emphasized the centrality of the role of the church's prayer within in the community of believers, as well as its inaccessibility to

it is true that the liturgy is something done by believers and not nonbelievers—and this is clear even *a priori* from the "political correctness" of every good, modern society—it is also true that reflection on the truth of the liturgical act began right from the start not by a consideration of "political evidence" but with theological evidence, according to which faith precedes liturgy or according to which, to cite Pajano again, "participation in the liturgy demands conversion." Would precisely this be *Sacrosanctum Concilium's point of arrival*?

In reality, we still must turn our perspective upside down: while it may be true that recent studies have offered an ecclesiastical history of the liturgical movement, and it may also be true that the historical account offered by these same studies is unconvincing, we must say that, in both cases, the principle problem is *the failure to comprehend the theological profundity of the liturgical movement, of its most fundamental and audacious*

---

those without faith" (26). Here is evident liturgical theology's long opposition to the primacy of doctrine over rite (of *lex credendi* over *lex supplicandi*) that was *one of the obstacles that the liturgical movement sought to overcome*, and not for political reasons, but for authentically theological reasons, as the preceding chapters have sought to demonstrate.

The presentation of this "reason" is offered as if one of the sweetest fruits of the liturgical movement were not precisely that of having contributed to the new understanding of revelation and faith, radically connecting both to liturgy, no longer conceiving worship as *protestatio* of a *fides* already possessed but as a fundamental and irreducible part of the very *actus fidei*. For an exploration of this relationship between *intellectus fidei* and *intellectus ritus* in the liturgical movement, cf. A. Grillo, "Intellectus fidei und intellectus ritus: Die überraschende Konvergenz von Liturgietheologie, Sakramententheologie und Fundamentaltheologie," *Liturgisches Jahrbuch* 50 (2000): 143–65.

aspirations, of its radical discovery of the liturgical act as fons of the church's life. This insight, which permeates this book, helps us formulate a better historical account of the liturgical movement.

It is well known, up to now, that the liturgical movement consists of two great phases:

The *first phase* extends from 1909, from the "Malines event,"[17] to 1947, the year of the publicaton of the encyclical *Mediator Dei,* the first document in church history to make the liturgical dimension of faith the object of magisterial teaching. These first forty years of the movement were dominated by research surrounding the liturgical question, wholly oriented toward offering a solution that took account first of all of the value of *initiation into the rites.* The result of this work was the gradual discovery of the need for *reform of the rites.* But, we can almost say, this first phase of the liturgical movement identified a question and proposed a dual solution, subordinating reform to initiation. It identified reform as an instrument intended to help bring about the great work of making the ritual logic of the Christian faith more broadly accessible.

A *second phase* extended from 1947 to 1988, twenty-five years after *Sacrosanctum Concilium* and, more symbolically, *one generation* from the Council.[18] The

[17] [The reference is to the National Congress of Catholic Action, held in Malines, Belgium, in 1909. At that gathering, Dom Lambert Beauduin delivered an influential address in which he insisted on active participation in the church's liturgical life as the true foundation of Christian living. This is frequently marked as the beginning of the liturgical movement. —Trans.]

[18] The year 1988 is a highly symbolic date, because it included three very different but very significant events: the promulgation of John Paul II's apostolic letter *Vigesimus quintus annus* on the

dynamic of the liturgical reform during these forty years was concentrated on theological doctrine and concrete pastoral development. This phase had a double end. On the one hand, it produced—through much hard work and often marked by great prophetic results—a series of *new rituals* that ensured the celebrative base for a new era in the life of the church. By concentrating on this aspect of the solution to the liturgical question, however, the urgency of the challenge of initiating the people into the liturgy was reduced. In fact, one of the results of this second phase—despite the intentions of the reformers—was to change the accents and the priorities of the movement. *Reform was no longer seen as an instrument of initiation; rather, initiation was seen as an instrument (often understood as a gradual) for the reform.*

To these two phases, however, we must add a third, one that it is that still largely in progress.

A *third phase* begins, broadly, in 1988 and extends up to today and into the future. Its precise nature is not yet entirely clear, but it promises a return of attention to the dimension of "initiation into the liturgy," with all that this entails. This might appear at first glance to contradict in some way the reform of the rites, almost a repudiation or a turning back, a problematic "reform of the reform."[19] In this phrase, "reform of the reform,"

---

occasion of the twenty-fifth anniversary of *Sacrosanctum Concilium*, the Lefebvrian schism, and the approval of the Roman Rite for the Diocese of the Congo.

[19] For an interesting consideration of the relationship between "progress" and "regress," not only for praxis and for the liturgical reform, but above all for "liturgical thought," see A. Cardita, "¿Progreso o retroceso de la teologia liturgica? Elementos para una re-

one sees above all a clear narrowing of perspective in how the liturgical question is understood and in a possible response in terms of the liturgical renewal. If everything that is not reform is perceived as a negation of the reform, we risk falling into having to make a fictional choice: either reform or return to the past. On the contrary, the "other issue of the reform"—foreseen by Guardini while the Council was still in session—is that *because* of the reform, and *in a way that does not contradict* its rites and texts, the more fundamental and structural question of "liturgical form," of "liturgy as *fons*," be addressed, and this suggests for the church a fundamental need for education, formation, and initiation into the act of worship.[20]

For this reason, it is time to return today to the "other issue," the other aspect of the liturgical question, bringing to light the inevitable "initiation" to which the new rites call us. In other words, and programmatically, we can say: *The reform of the books and rites, of the texts and gestures, is a necessary condition, but not in itself sufficient, for an authentic experience of the liturgy as* fons. What is necessary is a reemergence of the most fundamental concerns of the liturgical

---

flexiòn epistemològica sobre 'Liturgie de Source' de Jean Corbon," *Revista catalana de Teologia* 26, no. 2 (2001): 337–64.

[20] Just prior to the Council, two great authors already recognized this problem as "the fundamental question." I refer to R. Guardini ("Lettera sull'atto di culto e il compito attuale della 'formazione liturgica,'" *Humanitas* 20 [1965]: 85–90) and G. Dossetti (*Per una «chiesa eucaristica». Rilettura della portata cottrinale della Costituzione liturgica del Vaticano II. Lezioni del 1965*, ed. G. Alberigo and G. Ruggieri [Bologna: Il Mulino, 2002]). The prophetic value of these witnesses is today highly useful in overcoming any theological and pastoral embarrassment with regard to Christian rites.

movement and the liturgical thinking of the beginning of the twentieth century, when authors like Festugière and Beauduin, Guardini and Casel, discovered the fundamental nature of the liturgy as *source*, its belonging to the *act of faith* itself, and its place in the very heart of Christian revelation.

I think that a reconsideration of this historical vision can be very instructive, above all in interpreting the most controversial and important aspects of the debate on the liturgy today, which too often amounts to an unreasonable *laudatio temporis acti*[21]—whether it be of the Second Vatican Council or the Council of Trent does not matter—that is indifferent to the most radical meaning of the liturgical question. In the end, both the defending to the death of the liturgical reform and the efforts to "reform the reform" are both tendencies that end in the same error, that is, in a failure to consider the delicate equilibrium between reform of the rites and initiation into the rites, which can never be resolved one way or the other, neither by reforming without initiating nor by initiating without reforming.[22]

[21] [A classical Latin phrase meaning a praising of times past or of "the good old days." —Trans.]

[22] The consideration to which we subject the liturgical movement in this study tends to show precisely this *interweaving* of a logic of Initiation and a logic of the Reformation at the very foundation of the movement. It is just this "liturgical question," claiming precisely this radical connection, that preoccupied all of the authors of the *first phase* of the liturgical movement (that is, Festugière, Beauduin, Casel, Guardini, Parsch, and perhaps Guéranger himself).

4. THE TWO MEANINGS OF *RESSOURCEMENT*

In light of what we have said, we can now consider the meaning of the great *ressourcement*, typically understood as a "return to the sources" of the Christian faith. Certainly, it is a return to the sources of the liturgy, but this was oriented—at least in its great beginnings—to the rediscovery of the liturgy as source. The "source" in question is never simply a written text but an act of worship. And the theological contribution of the twentieth-century liturgical movement was essentially the rediscovery of the ritual action of the liturgy as the action of God and of humanity and therefore as "source" of the experience of faith and "source" of theological reflection. This "source," clearly, must be recovered by way of specific "sources." There are written sources and there are liturgical sources of the source that *is* the liturgy, but essentially it is the latter that must be recovered and that must guide research.

When we confuse these various types of sources, we risk thinking that the "culture of the sources" ends at Tertullian, Ambrose, or Augustine (and specifically, with the words they wrote), rather than at our own act of worship (at the *res*) as source of faith and theology for our time. This is not to detract for a moment from the words of Ambrose or Augustine, so long as we remember that theirs is not the final word.

It is therefore essential to keep in mind that *ressourcement*—the "return to the sources" that initiated a new era of modern theological research—is not only a tool for rediscovering liturgy's own authenticity; it can also be a sign of a deficiency, a crisis, an experience of troubling inauthenticity in ritual worship. The "return to the sources" must lead us today, in clear ways, to the "sources of return": we will quickly discover that liturgy's essential role as *fons* is truly the fundamental issue that lies hidden behind the sudden historical development in liturgical and theological study.[23]

In the often superficial judgment of many today, however, it seems that the first result of this rediscovery of the "sources" was an immediate "crisis" of praxis. P. Sequeri expressed the idea well: "When the samurai who defends the village asks himself in bewilderment, 'What am I doing?' and he wonders about the meaning of his being there, or even about the relevance of being a samurai at all, these are questions that will paralyze action."[24] And "paralysis of action" means—for the samurai and for the liturgy— loss of self. In reality, no one has ever attempted such a radical rediscovery of the sources except in a situation of a grave crisis of praxis. *The crisis is not the effect but the cause of the* ressourcement. *And yet* ressourcement *cannot be the ultimate solution to this crisis.*[25]

---

[23] Some interesting reflections on the true significance of the concept of *ressourcement*—in particular in the fathers, but more generally for the very concept of *traditio*—is found in J. Ratzinger, "I Padri nella teologia contemporanea," in J. Ratzinger, *Natura e compito della teologia* (Milan: Jaca Book, 1993), 143–61. A certain tension between *ressourcement* and *aggiornamento* is inevitable and can never be completely resolved. In reality, it includes the concept of source and regards in a decisive way the role that one understands *liturgy* to have in this delicate balance between identity and relevance, past and future, repetition and novelty.

[24] P. Sequeri, *La presenza e il fare. Ritrattazioni filosofico-teologiche sul modello liturgico della coscienza credente*, in AA.VV., *L'arte del celebrare* (Rome: Ed. Liturgiche-CLV, 1999), 21–40.

[25] For this reason, I believe that one cannot understand the concept of *ressourcement* in terms too strongly philological or methodological if it is to be understood essentially as "return to the liturgy as source." The concept of *aggiornamento*, from this point of view,

For this reason, I would argue that the deeper historical awareness with regard to Christian liturgy has led us to two related challenges, rooted in its origins and reaching beyond itself. The crisis of the initiation of Christians into the rites and by means of the rites brought about a "return to the sources," which in turn prepared for and brought about a "reform." This reform can be brought to completion in Christian living only through an adequate liturgical initiation of believers into the Christian faith. We can say, in other words, that behind and before the "historical shift" that brought a new theological understanding of the rites through a "return to the sources," there is the pastoral question of their actual significance as "sources of the life of the church's faith."

How can we understand, then, what it means to say that the liturgy is "source"? Certainly many "sources," both ancient and modern, are helpful. Most exemplary in this regard is Odo Casel's proposal that, in *ressourcement*, ancient sources must always be accompanied by modern sources, ensuring "global thought," understood as the capacity for initiation into the liturgy as *fons* to open the Christian to a new kind of "participated" understanding, which Casel called "gnosi," based on the thought of the fathers but which philosophy and anthropology also helps to explain.[26]

---

is no different from the concept of the rediscovery of the liturgy as "source" of Christian experience and knowledge.

[26] E. Mazza rightly says ("L'iniziazione cristiana e la tradizione liturgica dei primi secoli," in AA.VV., *Il Battesimo dei bambini*, 107–42, soprattutto 111–12) that Casel is not rigorous in applying the historical method because he is too much a theologian and a philosopher. I think, however, that we must ask whether the historical

In the final analysis, I repeat that ressourcement *is not simply a renewed attention to the "sources," but rather the tireless attempt to articulate again—but in a different way—in what sense the liturgy is source.*

5. THE TWO MEANINGS OF LITURGICAL REFORM

In light of what has been said, we can now come to a sort of final inversion of the terms with which we ordinarily think about the liturgical reform. Until now, it has commonly been thought that a reform of the church brings a reform of the rites. That is, new information, new ideas, new insights, new theological discoveries all call for the church to celebrate the God of Jesus Christ in a way that is more coherent with the new vision, more adapted and updated, as well as more faithful and authentic.

But what is the meaning of the *aggiornamento* of which the Council spoke? Precisely here we must think in a different direction. The reform of the church called for by the Council begins with what liturgical worship brings about—as *fons*—in the understanding of the church's faith. The new status of participation in the sacrament—in its identity as symbolic-ritual structural mediation—comes because the "liturgical reform" is not first of all about a need for modifying the rites; rather, it is about the way the ritual celebration promises to modify the life of the church. The rediscovery of

---

method (the "correct" one) only finds in "historical data" what it believes to be important "systematically"—if only on an implicit and unspoken level—as a prerequisite and condition of its historical investigation. Reflection on this aspect of the question belongs constitutively to the liturgical movement and to liturgical studies.

the initiatic dimension of the liturgical rite—with all its peculiarities of Word and of Sacrament—therefore constitutes a "promise of the reform" that is still largely unexplored. In this sense, then, the liturgical reform does not mean first of all the reform of the liturgy and its rites that is carried out by the church but rather *the reform of the church that is carried out by the liturgy and its rites*. But this cannot happen without a new awareness of liturgy as *fons* and of the initiatic dimension of participation that it demands, along the lines that we have sketched here and that we have seen appearing on the horizon of research and contemporary practice.

Only this outdated aspect of the reform, I am convinced, can make it truly relevant today, while the various attempts to make it relevant only serve inevitably to hollow it out, leading in nostalgic and irrational directions, offering fatuous support to a nonsensical "reform of the reform" that has no interest in continuing the journey of the liturgical movement but would just as soon pretend it had never happened. The courage to be "outdated" in this way is the key to being faithful to the history of the reform and not taking flight from it, either into a traditionalism that is only the death of tradition or a progressivism that wants to repeat the liturgical reform in every generation, resulting in both the reform and the liturgy itself coming to naught.

Two generations into the reform called for by *Sacrosanctum Concilium*, people who have no personal experience of the previous "liturgical regime," who have never celebrated a Mass in Latin, and who have never seen or lived the pomp and the rigidity of the preconciliar celebrations, now begin to reflect systematically on the liturgy. To these generations of Christians, it might seem that the reform was not sufficiently thought through, or perhaps that it was thought through, but not with them in mind.[27]

Its language, in fact, communicates and makes sense only to one who already knows the traditional liturgical workings. Thus, the reform caused two different and concomitant events: it renewed the praxis of worship, but it also took away the context that explains the reform itself. Only in the traditional experience can one find the context for an appropriation of the liturgy by the new generation. But it is not even possible that the loss of this tradition by "recent Christians" can be recovered simply by means of archaeological or philological explorations. The study of the liturgy in the historical-philological sense confirms only one part of the need that the Council indicated.

All the work of studying the past can only be a preparation for the new experience that must come about in the postconciliar generation: all of the study of the *sources* serves only to rediscover the *liturgy as source*. As long as we have to "explain" the Christian symbols, it will mean that they still lack new life and energy and that they are still empty. *The lack of the necessary immediacy of the experience of worship is one of the great problems that faces the church of the third millennium.* If we are unable to find adequate categories for effective access to our celebrations, then we are in a situation in which the

---

[27] Of great interest in evaluating the impact of the liturgical reform on the different generations is the brief but important essay by G. Remondi, "I 'santi segni' della riforma della messa," *Vita monastica* 55 (2001): 49–61. One discovers, with a certain pleasant surprise, how quickly the reconfigured elements of the liturgy have become quite obvious and taken for granted, less than forty years after the changes.

"people of God" have lost the possibility of finding—though certainly with effort—the *pleasure* and the *consolation* of celebrating. And that will mean the end of that beginning of rediscovery of the unfathomable depths of Christian liturgy but also inevitably the beginning of the end of a truly adult Christianity.

Still, what Beauduin noted in 1914 remains true—and offers special comfort: "Generations of people have spent centuries unlearning the traditional piety (that is, the liturgy): they will spend centuries relearning it." And we are just a century from these words, and only forty years from the reform.

Now, given all of this, it is obvious that the liturgical movement is not the *longa manus* of a papacy that does not want to miss the (last?) train for the christianization of society; nor is it simply the preparation of the (truly fertile?) ground on which the Council planted the liturgical reform. Neither of these visions—inspired by the idea of "conquering secularization" or "reforming premise/promise"—fully grasp the truth of the "birth of the liturgy in the twentieth century," that is, the complex attempt to provide an answer to a *liturgical question* that is perceived as a crisis of the meaning of the Christian rites both in the eyes of culture and in the eyes of faith. The great storehouse of the liturgical movement was only partially unpacked by the reform, leaving behind its most fundamental aspect, that of initiation into the liturgy. But then again, how can we think that a reform can ever decide its own initiation?[28]

---

[28] It would basically be like thinking that the author of a play can predetermine and prejudge—in the text—things that only the context of the *performance* can determine. The ritual book, important

For this reason, one can say that the liturgy was *born* in the twentieth century, because for the first time it became the object of direct, immediate, and almost voracious theological interest. Its nature as *fons* of the entire life of the church—brought to light with great suffering and patience through work that was first done underground and then in the sunlight of the liturgical movement—today calls for a quantum leap, a new and honest simplicity, a meticulous respect for the "data" and the liturgical "phenomenon" as such. *Only in this way can the reform be not only the reform that the church and Christians make of the liturgy but also the reform that the liturgy makes of the church and of Christians.*

6. A BRIEF SUMMARY IN SEVEN THESES

As we conclude these considerations, having considered the various fundamental aspects of the *"outdated relevance"* of the liturgical movement, let us summarize in an orderly way the fundamental points that emerge.

1. The liturgical movement proposes and practices a new theological method that refutes the antithesis between anthropology and theology. The very structure of ritual Christian action demands a synthesis, not an opposition, between the action of God and the action of persons. This is quite

---

as it is, will always be *just a book*, not a *rite* with all its richness of codes and language, space and time, relations and silences, things said and not said. For a careful reflection on this question, mixed with delightful historical-biographical notes, see C. Valenziano, *La Riforma Liturgica del Concilio. Cronaca teologia arte* (Bologna: EDB, 2004).

clear in the thinking of M. Festugière, R. Guardini, O. Casel, and P. Parsch.

2. One cannot understand the liturgical movement as a "theological shift" as opposed to an "anthropological shift." Rather, one must recognize in it a new theological method, which can be described as a "theology of the second anthropological shift." This method refers to the human person in a nonintellectualistic way and incorporates the attention to the sensible that developed as a result of the linguistic and phenomenological shift.

3. One must recognize that the response that the liturgical movement offers to the liturgical question is drawn from both of these "anthropological shifts" but with an important difference: in fact, the first anthropological shift offers a solution to the liturgical question that is still essentially intellectualistic, while the second shift proposes a solution that is essentially symbolic, historical, phenomenological, and relational. We can say that the first shift inspires a response primarily in terms of reform, while the second shift inspires a response in terms of initiation.

4. The liturgical movement is divided into three great phases. In the first, the dominant element was initiation into the rites themselves. In the second, reform of the rites prevailed. In the third and final reform, a new equilibrium is needed, rediscovering the movement's vocation to initiation. In this perspective, the reform is a necessary condition, but an insufficient one, for responding to the liturgical question.

5. The relevance of the liturgical movement consists, therefore, in its "outdatedness." We must

propose today a reconsideration of *the use and the abuse of the reform for the liturgy.* We might well be misunderstood. We might be applauded by the right and jeered by the left. But it is certain that if the liturgical movement has been thought until now to be a preparation for the reform, we must realize and insist that the blessed reform was only a preparation for the liturgical movement. The "work of the Spirit," we must not forget, is not merely the reform of the rites; it is the liturgical movement itself.

6. The (objective) *use* of the reform is that it is an indispensible tool to return the liturgy to its role as *fons* of the entire life of the church. The (potential) *abuse* consists, on the other hand, in leaving no space for an initiation of which the rites are not the object but the subject. The reform is, in fact, an operation in which the liturgy is (inevitably) only object. Liturgical initiation, of which the reform is an instrument, allows the liturgy to be *fons* and subject.

7. All of this means, finally, the discovery of a more fruitful—and fundamentally clear—relationship between reform of the liturgy and reform of the church. In short, we believe that the liturgical reform is essentially that renewal *whose subject is the church and whose object is the rites,* but perhaps the most prophetic intuition of the liturgical movement is the rediscovery that *the real subject of the liturgical reform is the liturgy and the real object is the church.*

Is there something "outdated" about this thinking today? And is there not, therefore, an urgent need today to rediscover, before all else, the prophetic, uncomfortable, and audacious "irrelevance" of the liturgical movement in order to remain faithful to the reform and never forget its true meaning?

7. FIVE EXAMPLES TO CLARIFY THE CHALLENGES OF THE LITURGICAL MOVEMENT TODAY

We cannot conclude this historical and theoretical consideration of the intentions of *Sacrosanctum Concilium* without connecting the historical-theological theory to the liturgical-sacramental practice of the church. In this final section, I wish to offer some examples of the ways that *Sacrosanctum Concilium*'s recovery of the liturgy's fundamental status as *fons et culmen* can impact our actual liturgical praxis.

It is often said, for example, that what was once a poverty for the Word of God in Catholic experience has been satisfied—perhaps too much. We now have—primarily in the eucharistic celebration but also in the celebration of the other sacraments—easier access to the Word with the help of the famous "missalette" or "worship aid." And this certainly had a highly positive role following the Council in developing a new mentality. Then there is the more frequent possibility of receiving Communion under two forms. On a third level, we have a great deal more information on the ritual details of the sacraments, such as the eschatological meaning of being dressed in a white garment during the rite of baptism. We are strongly committed to a catechetical process for children that calls for the sacramental succession of *baptism–first confession–first Communion–confirmation*, and finally, among our pastoral concerns is the question of the place within the ecclesial community of those who are divorced and remarried.

These are five liturgical-pastoral experiences that seem clear enough on the surface. But within each one we find a powerful level of contradiction between the intentional dimension (the meaning) and the functional dimension (the sign/ritual symbol). I seek briefly to shed some light on these below.

Reading or Hearing the Word?

We begin by asking in what way the informative reading of a missalette can happen at the same time as the symbolic hearing of the Word. This is a point on which behavior very often contradicts what we in fact want (or, better, need) to experience. The fact that I control (with my eyes) the text in the missalette prevents me from hearing it (with my ears): I read instead of listening, and this gets in the way of the experience of communion that is essential to "hearing the Word."

This can be addressed aggressively, insisting on a need for change, but pastorally it must be approached slowly. Yet it must be approached, and not ignored, because otherwise we are left for four or five generations with the contradiction between intention and reality. And functional reality, the pre-intentional, normally drags down the intentional. This is an example of so-called nonverbal language sooner or later transforming verbal language. The "nonword"—that is, a word that I essentially control with my eyes—makes it impossible, over the course of three generations, for me to hear anything. This basic ritual action (that often becomes for us "nonaction") has a theoretical implication that ordinary pastoral ministry can no longer ignore. The proper place for the proclamation of the

Word is in the context of hearing together (and not reading together).

Communion "under Both Species" or Communion in the Bread and the Cup?

We come to the second point, which is still more delicate: the topic of the distribution of Holy Communion "under both species" from a linguistic point of view. Our way of talking about this still today is certainly classic, inasmuch as it is learned and refined, but it is still an unfortunate phrase, from the point of view of the reality to which we are referring. "Communicating under both species" is clearly a poor choice of words, because it says nothing about the act it describes or, better, speaks of the act in terminology borrowed from theological theories about the relationship between species and substance. The full meaning of the act to which "communicating under both species" refers consists in participating together in the bread broken and the cup shared.

Considering this act in its integrality and fullness, the practice of intinction—dipping the bread into the wine—also offers a strong form of symbolic reduction, because it gives preeminence to the bread and wine considered abstractly. That both species are technically included in Communion is not enough; the act is one of eating together the one bread broken and drinking together the one cup shared. Here too the good intention of leaving behind Communion with only the one species of bread and the way it was accomplished introduce a tension between the intentional dimension and the pre-intentional dimension, between the voluntary and the involuntary, that prevents the act of Communion from being truly *fons*. In reality, we can only accept that that act is *fons*, on a level other than rhetorically, to the extent that we can still respect its nature as symbolic-ritual action. This challenge was discovered anew, with respect to the post-Tridentine praxis, barely one hundred years ago, in all its undeniable sacramental and ecclesial urgency.

What about the White Garment of Baptism?

The third example is more autobiographical, and I offer it as an episode of lived experience. The issue of the white garment used in the baptismal rite is one about which I care deeply, because unless you have presented your own child for baptism, you might not realize the remarkable example of pastoral sleight of hand that is often involved. I refer to the way that a white garment is taken from a drawer in the church sacristy, pulled out at the right moment during the baptism, placed on the baby while the proper formula is recited, and then placed back in the drawer!

If there is more than one child being baptized, it is placed on one of them, then on the others one by one, and then put back in the drawer, ready for the next time the solemn rites are performed. The babies are not even dressed in the garment; it is just held over them as though part of a superstitious rite—and then back to the drawer it goes. It is not worn and it does not become *that* child's vestment.

This means entering the rite only as far as the ritual demands it, and no farther. The rubrics do not say what we have to do with the garment, so it goes back in the drawer. From a rubrical point of view, it makes perfect sense, but in reality it fails to enter into the logic of the rite. Underneath lurks a powerful theology, according to which what counts is *knowing the mean-*

ing of what we do: when the meaning is understood, the gesture, the sign, no longer has any purpose. All that counts is intention. The pre-intention in certain cases is contradictory, and in other cases I can make it disappear, so much so that many say that it is enough to think about the meaning, while the sign is superfluous. Many parish priests confess calmly and carelessly of being able to (or having to) move beyond this whole business of signs.

What Is the Order for the Christian Initiation of Children?

More radical, and much thornier, is the problem of the loud contradiction between the Christian initiation of children that we ordinarily and necessarily feel we must follow and the functional meaning of the ritual actions we celebrate. We might half-jokingly say that we celebrate four sacraments (baptism, first confession, first Communion, confirmation) and of the four, not one of them is in the right place! Well, one of them is: baptism, because, as von Balthasar said, the baptism of infants is one of the most consequential decisions in the history of the church. It is done and it will continue to be done, but we must be aware that the practice is a luxury that we allow ourselves only under certain conditions.

The fact that before first Communion we celebrate first confession—against all appreciable canonical logic—is and will remain a contradiction. There can be a first confession only *after* first Communion. If there must be a first confession, it must be before the second Communion, not before the first! And the first Communion cannot be before confirmation, because at least on the rhetorical level we emphasize the fact that we arrive at the sacramental pinnacle with first Communion, and yet after that we still lack something. But then we have to ask, which is more important? And the perception is that when we reach confirmation, administered by the bishop, we have truly reached the culminaton of Christian initiation, but this is absolutely false.

The little door through which our ordinary praxis is stuck is an exceptional circumstance of history: that is, the lack of availability of the bishop to celebrate it often. We have allowed an exception to become an ordinary, structured, pastoral program, thinking that formation can determine the sacraments rather than the sacraments determining formation, precisely in the form and in the ritual process with which they are celebrated.

The Sacraments and "Irregular Situations"
of Married Christians

We have reached the final point—but in this point we see clearly the heart of the theory that I have tried to demonstrate in each of the other examples above. I refer to the issue of people who have divorced and remarried. The problem is surely complex. Those who suggest that there is only an appearance of complexity, due to the church's backward attitudes and nothing more, are mistaken. The position of divorced and remarried people in the church is a grave and burning question, provided one accepts that the sacramental practice of the church is neither ornamental nor marginal, for at base the problem is truly resolved only at the sacramental level, not the juridical level, except by way of exception. Without prejudice to the juridical way, the ordinary way must be a penitential one. And yet today, there is no thought given to a penitential journey for the divorced and remarried.

The true problem, which is only marginally juridical, is the difference between ecclesial communion and sacramental communion. It is true that a divorced and remarried couple are not excommunicated from the church. Fine. The problem, however, is that, if their position of difference between ecclesial communion and sacramental communion is permanent, the church places itself in a crisis that cannot be overcome. There can be a long period of difference between sacramental communion and ecclesial communion, but there must be for everyone the possibility of seeing full communion restored.

If we say to someone, "You are part of the church, but you can never have sacramental communion," in truth we risk falling into a form of grave hypocrisy. I understand that there are delicate questions of principle. But the basic meaning of ecclesial belonging being linked to sacramental communion means that while we might say to a baptized person, "You are sentenced to thirty years of penance," we can never say, "You are given a life sentence." From an ecclesial point of view, there can be no life sentence. It is also an absurd claim canonically. Yet pastorally we take refuge in saying, "But they are part of the church." This would ultimately mean that one can be part of the church independently of the sacraments, that there could be some ecclesial belonging without an *authentic* sacramental, baptismal, and eucharistic dimension.

8. CONCLUSION

This is the "liturgical question" that we must respond to today, thanks to *Sacrosanctum Concilium* and following beyond it, along the rich and complex journey that is what I have called the third phase of the liturgical movement. And in order to remain faithful to the third phase, we can never forget the admonition of Paul VI that is presented as the introductory epigraph of this chapter and that we return to here, as an even more fitting conclusion: "The hour has come, it seems to us, in which the truth about the Church of Christ must be explored, ordered, and expressed, perhaps not with those solemn statements that are dogmatic definitions, but with declarations by which the Church, with more explicit and authoritative teaching, declares what it thinks about itself."

Among these forms of "more authoritative declarations," the liturgical act of worship—in its symbolic-ritual concreteness—is perhaps the most delicate and the most fundamental. With symbolic-ritual authority such as this, the church—today, as fifty years ago—can do no more and no less.

Chapter 4

The Liturgical Reform: Necessary but Insufficient

> Fatal human pride! The devil's exaltation of intellect, which imagines itself to contain all good, and which is ignorant that knowledge is but a slender and elementary principle of good; and that that which is truly and perfectly good belongs to genuine action, to effective will, and not to a merely intellectual process! And yet this *pride of intellect* has been until now the perpetual snare of mankind.[1]
>
> —Antonio Rosmini

The hopes that the liturgical reform generated within the church fifty years ago were judged from the start, by a small minority, as a sort of dangerous fantasy. A half century later, these same hopes remain illusive and uncertain, seeming at times to be the product of delusion or blind stubbornness. And so it is worth asking: Were those whom Pope John dismissed as "prophets of doom" correct after all?

In providing an answer, I do not want to resort to language that sounds—especially for a conscientious

---

[1] A. Rosmini, *Delle cinque piaghe*, 11, 125, italics mine. [ET: Antonio Rosmini, *Of the Five Wounds of the Holy Church*, ed. H. P. Liddon (London: Rivingtons, n.d., originally published 1846), 10. —Trans.]

objector to military service like me—too militant. But the reason for the militant defense of the reform that I offer here is—though carefully attentive to the demands and expectations of scholarly work—to revive the lost hopes that I am convinced still merit sustenance and nourishment.

The path I shall follow in this chapter is simple, almost linear. It begins with the idea articulated in the chapter title: the fact that the reform was considered necessary does not mean that it was intended to be an end in itself. By identifying its necessity with its sufficiency, we have lost sight of the purpose and proportions of the reform, satisfied with a few technical adjustments but ignoring its substantial meaning. And so we have allowed ourselves to become victims of the very formalism that so many worked so hard to overcome.

To distinguish the necessity of the reform from its sufficiency can be done only by way of *a profound reconsideration of "the liturgical question" as foundation and motive of the liturgical movement.* Our understanding of the relationship between the liturgical movement and the liturgical reform needs to be corrected, even turned upside down. *We can no longer understand the liturgical movement as a cause and liturgical reform as its effect. Rather—and surprisingly—the liturgical reform is the cause and the liturgical movement is its effect!* This point of view helps us to see the liturgical movement no longer as a past event but as one that remains in our present and also a part of the promising future that lies ahead of the church.

This chapter is, if you will, a sort of symphony, made up of four brief movements. First, I will clarify what the forgotten "liturgical question" actually is, because we must remember it and understand how it could ever have been so easily forgotten (the first movement of the symphony: *allegro ma non troppo*). This will make clear that the liturgical movement began as a response to the liturgical question and is the result of the need for a new method for theology and pastoral ministry. These aims brought about, in a new liturgical-spiritual structure (*actuosa participatio*), the center of a pastoral transformation that happened in two movements: a new "liturgical initiation/formation" and a "liturgical reform." The reform was necessary as an instrument of the initiation/formation, and the initiation/formation was primary with respect to the reform. But this analysis runs against some indisputable evidence: *so much effort has been dedicated to the reception of the reform and very little to the reception of the formation/initiation*. From here, we turn to the task of understanding in a new way the classic triple identifying aspects of the sacraments: form-matter-minister (the second movement: *adagio cantabile a tre voce*) and to the dual possibility of "despair" and "presumption" that threatens liturgical hope when the relationship between the liturgical question and the liturgical movement is misunderstood (the third movement: *scherzo*).

Finally, we must understand the liturgical movement no longer as the *preamble* to the Council or of the reform but as *the context of them both*, theoretically and practically. Council and reform represent only one moment—the second phase—of the liturgical movement, though each had significant impact on the movement as a whole. Remembering now, in the third phase of the liturgical movement, what that movement was all about from the start will allow us to draw some reliable, though in some ways ironic, conclusions (the fourth movement: *rondo un poco capriccioso*).

1. THE DIFFICULT MEMORY OF THE LITURGICAL QUESTION (*ALLEGRO, MA NON TROPPO*)

As we have learned over many years now, the ways we understand the history of the Christian liturgy derive from ideas about it that were developed during the twentieth century. One of these is the idea that liturgical history can be divided into "dark ages" (from the end of the Middle Ages up until recently) and "golden ages" (the age of the early church and our own). This thinking, now more than fifty years old, represents a real scandal in our historical consciousness. It has compromised our understanding of the liturgical reform, the liturgical act, and the place of liturgy in the life of the church. With it has come a distressing level of archaeologism and an ecclesiological nostalgia. Correcting this serious error means recovering the theoretical horizon that gave rise to the liturgical movement as a response to the liturgical question and as the context of the process of reform/formation of the church with respect to its rites.

The argument I present here begins from a dual observation. Considered on its own, as we have already noted, the fruits of the liturgical reform have fallen far short of what was expected fifty years ago. On the other hand, this initial judgment seems all the more fragile when one forgets that *the liturgical reform is only one part of the response to the liturgical question*. False opinions and grave misunderstandings on this point abound today. The great era of the Second Vatican Council was based on more than fifty years of work within the liturgical movement. But this relationship between *receptio* and *institutio* was too quickly forgotten. That has produced a double misunderstanding.

On the one hand, many have been fooled into believing that the reform itself resolved the liturgical question. All that remains, in this view, is to defend the reform, and the game is won! *On the other hand*, the same blunder led others to believe that their criticism of liturgical reform necessarily means denying the liturgical question itself: only a "reform of the reform" can reestablish the true meaning of Christian worship. Both of these approaches *have in common the same dangerous prejudice*—namely, the idea that there is no liturgical question to justify either the liturgical movement or the liturgical reform that followed it, and that therefore the relationship between faith and ritual worship is self-explanatory, today just as it was in 1947 or 1870!

This, however, distorts not only contemporary ecclesial experience—which has what I would call a physiological need to return to the liturgy as source—but also liturgical studies itself, which developed in the last century specifically with the aim of providing a response to this question.

For this reason it seems to me that understanding the liturgical question in its pastoral dimension demands a careful and well-equipped approach to liturgical studies. But having the right care and equipment means approaching the task with a strong and urgent pastoral question, a profound rethinking of faith in the light of the rite and of the rite in the light of faith, and adequate instruments to enable an effective response.

The liturgical movement developed precisely on these two fronts: it profoundly and fundamentally reconsidered the role of symbolic-ritual worship in pastoral ministry and contemporary theology, but it had to utilize new instruments precisely in order to be able truly allow the rite to speak. The liturgical movement was therefore able, at the same time, to rethink "theological method" and to recover "foreign" fields of study such as anthropology, putting them to use in the service of the new method, in order to reach a new understanding of its object. This *shift* was invented not by Rahner or Chauvet or Bonaccorso but rather by men like Festugière, Guardini, and Casel. It introduced into theology what M. Merleau-Ponty described well as the duty to "broaden our reasoning":

> [A]nthropology's concern is neither to prove that the primitive is wrong nor to side with him against us, but to set itself up on a ground where we shall both be intelligible without any reduction or rash transposition. . . . Thus our task is to broaden our reasoning to make it capable of grasping what, in ourselves and in others, precedes and excedes reason.[2]

This brought for theology and for pastoral ministry a profound change of view and of priorities. This was already clear before *Sacrosanctum Concilium*, when at the inauguration of the second session of the Second Vatican Council, a Paul VI fresh from his election as bishop of Rome made the important statement that we have already noted above:

> The hour has come, it seems to us, in which the truth about the Church of Christ must be explored, ordered, and expressed, perhaps not with those solemn statements that are dogmatic definitions, but with declarations by which the Church, with more explicit

---

[2] M. Merleau-Ponty, "Da Mauss a Claude Lévi-Strauss," in M. Merleau-Ponty, *Segni* (Milan: il Saggiatore, 1967 [orig. ed. 1960]), 154–68, here 164. [ET: Maurice Merleau-Ponty, "From Mauss to Claude Lévi-Strauss," in Maurice Merleau-Ponty, *Signs* (Evanston, IL: Northwestern University Press, 1964), 114–25, here 122. —Trans.]

and authoritative teaching, declares what it thinks about itself.[3]

In light of these affirmations we can understand how the liturgical movement profoundly transformed classical theology's method of understanding, recovering the fundamental value of the symbolic-ritual action in the church's understanding of its own act of faith. The liturgical reform would come only following that, as a tool for acheiving this objective.

2. THE REFORM OF THE SACRAMENTAL TRIAD: FORM, MATTER, MINISTER (*ADAGIO CANTABILE A TRE VOCI*)

From what we have just said, it is clear that we must distingish well between three different dimensions—almost three *rationes*—of approach to and consideration of the liturgy. They are written into our common history, each influencing the other, and we must be able to take account of them when we deal with a question like that of the liturgical reform of the church. These dimensions are different, sometimes alternative, but they often overlap and even contradict each other. We shall briefly consider each individually and in a special way for *the particular experience of the time* that they enable us to understand better. In fact—we must acknowledge it—to resolve the question of the liturgical reform of the church means having already resolved the more general question of the awareness of different aspects and different depths that time acquires in these different modalities of experience of the liturgy.

---

[3] Pope Paul VI, Opening of the Second Session of the Second Vatican Council, September 29, 1963.

The Spiritual-Personal (Subjective) Dimension

The first dimension—or *ratio*—concerns the experience that the ecclesial subject (lay person, priest, or monastic) has of the liturgy. The subject's time—time that is fully one's own, time to be used well, to dedicate oneself to various efforts, to sacrifice—is stretched *ad libitum* over every celebration. It is clear, though, that here the totalization of time (the inclination to perpetual adoration or to repeated and continual celebration) is largely a result of the *assimilation of liturgical time and subjective time*. The desire for a symphony of celebration in subjective time (even though completely without foundation, of course, but extremely dangerous if absolutized) leads inevitably to a drift toward understanding it primarily as *exercise, asceticism, duty*. It is time "invested" and "quantitatively calculable," from which one expects—deep down—a return. It is time of "work" or of "study," not time of "prayer."

The Juridical-Disciplinary (Objective) Dimension

One of the words that we used in the preceding point—*duty*—leads us to the second great experience of liturgy, which we can call the *juridical-disciplinary*. Here, the liturgy itself is at the center, understood as *institution, juridical function, ecclesial structure* that objectively obliges the individual and that arises (or, better, imposes itself) with an objective, homogenous, almost inexorable time, compared to the subject's temporality. Here, the objectivity of the form, matter, and minister, every temporal and spatial condition, every contingent character of action is swallowed up into an insignificant atemporality. If, in the first model, the subjective temporality ends up swallowing entirely the time of the sacrament, now in this second case the rite's objective time reduces the subject's time to *adi-aphoron*. In this vision, time is either imposed or irrelevant, but in either case it is subject to "bookkeeping" or the expectation of a "return."

The Liturgical-Sacramental (Intersubjective) Dimension

Along with these two perspectives, however—so different from each other and yet so similar in consequences—there is also a most important *symbolic-ritual* dimension of the liturgy. It is rooted in the irreducibility of the liturgical celebration to ordinary space-time. There is a celebratory dimension of every liturgy, so that its ritual symbolicity is understood to be *a different experience of space and time.* This is mainly due to the believer stepping outside of a logic of opposition between subject and object,[4] between subjective–free time and objective–imposed time, giving shape to a dimension of the *intersubjective* that can never be reduced to time as a "homogenous continuum."

The "New Paradigm" and Its Consequences
for a Definition of Sacrament

None of these three models are without some good foundation, of course. But what should surprise us is that, in the inevitable overlapping of these experiences, what results are imbalances, abuses, and severe disfigurements of the integral experience of ritual symbol:

a) The secret alliance between the first two experiences (subjective and objective), almost affirming the reciprocal claim that one is interlocutor of the other, in fact has the effect of displacing the third

[4] Cf. G. Bonaccorso, *Celebrare la salvezza. Lineamenti di liturgia* (Padua: EMP-Abbazia di S. Giustina, 2003), 19–26.

experience, making it invisible and literally unlivable. The drama of our ecclesial and sacramental condition is precisely this most dangerous equation between invisible and unlivable.

b) And yet, we must understand that it is precisely the celebrative experience—intersubjective and symbolic-ritual—that constitutes the concrete foundation on which the useful spiritual and institutional abstractions then become possible. But a liturgy reduced to the subjective/objective dialectic (in relationship between rights and duties) *always ends up either subjectively desired or objectively obliged precisely because it is never communally celebrated.*

c) What is created, then, is a strange combination of an objective obligation of continual celebration of the sacrament and the subjective ideal of (solely) spiritual communion. The subject does not know what to do with the object and, vice versa, the object literally prescinds from the subject. And this reciprocal exclusion of the subject by the object and the object by the subject seems to support the minimal demands of a decent liturgical experience.

Application of the Model to the Form/Matter/Minister Triad
The concern for "active participation" that characterized the liturgical reform allows for a new and more profound grasp—in fact, almost a complete transfiguration and transmutation—of three cardinal concepts according to which the sacraments were understood for almost a millennium: *form, matter, and minister.*[5] Let us consider briefly the ways they are transformed.

---

[5] Cf. J. Wohlmuth, "Vorüberlegungen zu einer theologischen Aesthetik der Sakramente," in *Liturgische Theologie. Aufgaben*

—*The form*, previously understood to be the *formula* (of the act), becomes a *verbal anaphoric form* (of the action of grace) and ultimately the *ritual form (verbal and nonverbal) of the entire celebration*.

—*The matter*, previously understood to be the *physical matter* (upon which the formula is spoken), becomes the *historical matter* (of the action of grace) of the sacrament and ultimately *the symbolic matter of the celebration*.

—*The minister* (of the act), previously understood primarily to be *the individual titular subject who speaks the form upon the matter*, becomes an ecclesial chorus that was previously only *formally involved* but now *acts and celebrates in a participated and articulated way as the full ritual demands*.

This brief rereading of the form/matter/minister triad can help us grasp better the sacramental and ecclesial rethinking that is currently happening in our understanding of "participated liturgy" as the final and crucial objective of the liturgical reform. We must rediscover in our own time that the form of such participation is ritual in nature, that the matter is primarily historical-symbolic, and that the minister is plural and communitarian, so that the role of presiding must always support (and never detract from) the ministerial nature of the entire church. If this is clear, it is evident that the "celebrating assembly" is not a threat to but rather a guarantee of ordained ministry—indeed, its true purpose.

systematischer Liturgiewissenschaft, ed. H. Hoping and B. Jeggle-Mez (Paderborn: Schöningh, 2004), 85–106.

3. HOPE, DESPAIR, AND PRESUMPTION IN THE LITURGICAL REFORM (*SCHERZO*)

Like every ecclesial experience, the liturgical reform has nurtured the hopes of some. But it has also tempted many to the dual vices of despair and presumption.[6] Since both of these sins negate the possibility of hope, it is worth pausing a moment to consider them.

Hope is negated by *despair* because when we demand absolute, visible evidence there is no space left for the possibility of that which cannot be seen. Falling prey to despair means refusing to consider anything that is not perceived fully by senses and that does not surrender completely to them. The opposite negation of hope is *presumption*. With presumption, the unseen future is regarded not as impossible but as easily and securely within one's grasp. To consider oneself in control of the future (presumption) or to be controlled by the future (despair)—these are two ways of missing the delicate and subtle logic of liturgical initiation. To be frozen by the future or to freeze it in the present constitute the fundamental impediments to entering into the logic of what it means to be "saved" and "chosen," to be the "living stones" that travel the paths of time with *the freedom of the children of God, for whom the past is not irreversible and the future is not unpredictable.*

There seems today to be a lack of hope in the liturgical reform, both among some young people who despair in new rites and presume that older rites better safeguarded the church (or at least what they imagine to be the true church) and among some older folks,

[6] "Deinde considerandum est de vitiis oppositis (ad spem). Et primo de desperatione, secundo de presumptione" (Thomas Aquinas, *Summa Theologica*, 2–2, 20, Intr.).

prophets of doom who are also in some cases prelates
of considerable influence. For both of these subjects,
albeit for different reasons, memories that are not real
result in an obstruction of vision and a weakening of
spirit. While the young presume things about a time
they did not live through themselves, those who are
older idealize their ecclesial infancy in a way that lacks
a sense of reality.[7] This leads to a nostalgia expressed in

[7] A demonstration *par excellence* of this regressive nostalgia for
Latin is found in the idea—more widespread than one might think
and often promoted by pastors with a thoughtless automatism—
that "the liturgical reform never abrogated the earlier rites" (that is,
the rites that were the fruit of the Tridentine reform). In reality, this
idea can only be defended by turning the burden of proof on its
head. It is the nostalgic promoters of the Tridentine Rite who must
demonstrate that it was never abrogated; it does not fall to those
who follow the tradition of the church by celebrating according
to the rites (those of Paul VI) which explicitly reformed the earlier
ones. If the rite of Paul VI is the fruit of the reform of the preceding rite, it is clear that, at the moment it was promulgated and put
in force, *the preceding rite was substituted with the new one. Otherwise, why was there a reform at all?* Another naive assertion—also
quite common—regards the ritual plurality that Trent permitted
and that Vatican II ought therefore to be able to permit as well. In
reality, this is only a fallacy, an instance of bogus reasoning. Trent
permitted the restoration of *Latin rites other than the Roman Rite,*
not a Roman Rite other than the one determined by Trent. In other
words, what Trent did, Vatican II also did. Reforming the Roman
Rite, it did not permit the existence of *another* Roman Rite. At best,
this allows for the use of the previous rite "by indult," as an exception to the rule—including the rule of common sense—according
to which there can be at any one time only one Roman Rite, one
Ambrosian Rite, one Hispanic Rite, one Gallican Rite, etc. For an
example of such specious reasoning, see A. Nichols, *Looking at the
Liturgy: A Critical View of Its Contemporary Form* (San Francisco:
Ignatius, 1997); and Alcuin Reid, ed., *Looking again at the Question of*

grave forms of presumptuous despair or, more often, of desperate presumption. We see this, for example, in the presumption that the liturgical reform that followed the Council not only preceded various difficulties of our day but also caused them. To listen to such diagnoses, which are instances of the fallacy of *post hoc ergo propter hoc*, one would think that if only the liturgical reform had never happened, everything would be fine.[8]

But both the young people and the old who fall into these errors—and we should note that there is less excuse for those who are older, for they have the benefit of both greater experience and greater responsibility—forget that the liturgical question was first posed more than fifty years before the Council began. To cultivate hope today means to remember that the liturgical question is older than we are, older than our generation but also older than our grandparents. Indeed, it is at least four generations old!

Those who speak today in this forgetful and dangerously naive way regarding such old and delicate problems call to mind the comment made by the poet

---

the Liturgy with Cardinal Ratzinger: Proceedings of the July 2001 Fontgombault Liturgical Conference (St Michaels Abbey, 2004).

[8] Even if there is a clear contradiction, at least for those traditionalist authors who still retain a glimmer of realism in the heat of argument, in an "ancient" Roman Rite that, in order to be usable, needs to be reformed! Thus, paradoxically, they acknowledge that the possibility of using the "Missal of Pius V" today would call for at least a reform of the lectionary, the calendar, and the sanctoral cycle in order to make them adaptable. But this is precisely what led to the Missal of Paul VI, and that was already done forty years ago, evidently when these authors were not looking. Cf. A. Nichols, *Looking at the Liturgy*, 119–21.

Shelley about an elderly relative: "He lost the art of communicating, but not, unfortunately, the gift of speech." They remind us too of the incisive comment made by the biblical scholar Paul Beauchamp on the pitfalls of reading Scripture: "The Bible, when one knows it poorly, ends up being reduced to a screen upon which one projects images of one's childhood."[9] Precisely this—and perhaps worse—befalls the liturgy too when it is managed and judged by clumsy hands and forgetful heads.

4. CONCLUSION: IN PRAISE OF THE TRUCK DRIVER OVER INTELLECTUAL ARROGANCE (*RONDÒ UN POCO CAPRICCIOSO*)

The reform of the liturgy, then, is a tool that is both absolutely necessary and insufficient for ensuring a return of the liturgy to its place as *fons* of *all the activity of the church*. Only in this way will the greatest aspiration of the reform ever be realized—not only that the liturgical rites are reformed by the church, but ultimately that the church is reformed by its liturgical rites. This goal is the reason we can speak of both the necessity and the insufficiency of the reform.

It is a mistake to suggest, in the name of an overly abstract method or "closed" content, that theology ought not respond to pastoral questions and problems. On the contrary, this is its only true role, and it must be carried out with tools and methods worthy of a task so precious and essential to the life of the church. I think a great part of our work at Sant'Anselmo[10] must be

---

[9] P. Beauchamp, *Salmi notte e giorno* (Assisi: Cittadella, 2002), 16.

[10] [That is, the Pontifical Athenaeum of Saint Anselm in Rome, where the author is professor of sacramental theology. —Trans.]

directed to fulfilling this duty. We have had many successes along these lines but know that we must continue still further in this direction.

Therefore, I would like to conclude this "symphony" in two ways: *a semi-serious little rhythm* followed by *an effective and monumental conclusion*. First, a little advice to the future liturgist and then, finally, a brief look at the "wound of the left hand" of our holy church, more than 180 years after the prophetic insights of Antonio Rosmini.

The semi-serious rhythm: a modest piece of advice to the liturgist of the future. One thing we have learned over the past fifty years is that an authentic response to the liturgical question cannot be reduced to the technical execution of the reform, however faithful it might be. A true "liturgist," an expert in ritual things, must be one who is in profound contact with "the things of the faith," with the worship of God in Christ, yes, but also with both feet planted firmly within the lived experience of benediction and praise, of supplication and the action of grace. With this in mind, I offer something I heard recently from a distinguished man of the church, responsible for the formation of the clergy in a large diocese of northern Italy, who offered, with beautiful irony, his formidable criterion in the formation of new ministers of worship: "No one should study liturgy," he said, "until they have spent at least ten years as a truck driver."

Obviously, *I don't really mean to propose that the institutes of liturgical study introduce a special preparatory decade of practical study* to be carried out not in classrooms and libraries but on the highways of the world. But maybe some of this kind of real-world experience would teach would-be liturgists—at every level and setting—not to make too much of their own thoughts and experiences, gestures and tastes, and to avoid approaches that are too high or abstract, too narrow or abstruse.[11] Such experience would enable them perhaps to keep in mind the variety of people who will be involved in the liturgies they lead or coordinate, to avoid every cliche, and so always to aim for "*non ad enuntiabile, sed ad rem*."[12]

I ask myself: what would become of our sacristies, not to mention our Vatican congregations, if such a criterion were imposed? What new life would enter into our celebration of the liturgy, and how would the celebration of the liturgy enter into our lives?

On the other hand, as you will already suspect, this call for the integration of the truck driver with the liturgist is meant to emphasize—in the form of paradox—not so much a subjective model of what it means to be a liturgist as a disciplinary method that is truly faithful to liturgy itself. Max Weber was correct

---

[11] Also from the point of view of language, to suggest today that the formation of future priests should include not only a good foundation of classic study of the Latin language—which is surely necessary and useful—but also a *practical celebrative Latin* is a form of abstraction from reality that can be a prelude to a "relativism" that moves not from facts to principles but from principles to "facts." It affirms a blind principle—priests should be able to celebrate Mass in Latin—as if history had stopped, the world still speaks Latin, and priests will be discussing the news, poetry, and sports in Latin. But what fantasy world are we talking about?

[12] [The reference is to the teaching of St. Thomas Aquinas: "*Actus credentis non terminatur ad enuntiabile, sed ad rem*" (cf. *Summa Theologica*, II^a–IIae q. 1 a. 2 ad 2). (That is, faith is not merely about truths about God being spoken or understood, but in God being experienced and embraced.) —Trans.]

to say, "In the field of science only he who is devoted *solely* to the work at hand has personality."[13] And is this not just as true for one who endeavors to study liturgy, yesterday as well as today? How long will it be before we truly conform our methods of study to what is demanded of the object of study rather than continue to bend the object to the arid subtleties of our method?

The monumental conclusion: to heal the "wound of the left hand." At the same time it seems that we must bear in mind the temptation that always comes with worship. Antonio Rosmini described it lucidly over 180 years ago when he identified "the wound in the left hand of holy Church" to be "the division between people and clergy at public worship." In fact, recognizing the problem of worship too frequently being reduced to a matter of simple theoretical or moral knowledge, Rosmini observed, "Fatal human pride! The devil's exaltation of intellect, which imagines itself to contain all good, and which is ignorant that knowledge is but a slender and elementary principle of good; and that that which is truly and perfectly good belongs to genuine action, to effective will, and not to a merely intellectual process! And yet this *pride of intellect* has been until now the perpetual snare of mankind."[14]

[13] M. Weber, *La scienza come professione*, in Max Weber, *Il lavoro intelletturale come professione* (Torino: Einaudi, 1966), 16. [ET: Max Weber, *From Max Weber: Essays in Sociology*, ed. and trans. H. H. Gerth and C. Wright Mills (New York: Oxford University Press, 1946), 137. —Trans.]

[14] A. Rosmini, *Delle cinque piaghe*, 11, 125, italics mine. [ET: Rosmini, *Of the Five Wounds of the Holy Church*, 10. —Trans.]

There is an intellectual arrogance that menaces the liturgical reform. It seems unable to escape from the logic of wanting to "find sources" of the liturgy, forgetting that the true *ressourcement* to be sought is for the liturgy to become again today (and, still better, tomorrow) the source of Christian life, the foundation of believers' thought and action, precisely because it knows how to be and to remain *symbolic-ritual action*.

To this aspiration of Rosmini—which remains, more than a century, the *desideratum* of the liturgical reform—I would like to restore life and hope. But such hope needs all of our audacity and patience. For the liturgists of tomorrow, it will mean working with the attentiveness of an artist and the wisdom of a truck driver, with ritual style and vital openness, with an acute sense of transcendence and an authentic enjoyment of humanity: with that synthesis between thought and life that Cypriano Vagaggini identified half a century ago as the most noble aspiration and concern of modern thought.

Precisely in this regard—and I say this almost in a whisper, though I would like to shout it out from the rooftops—I believe that to hope for and dream of a liturgy that is open to life and modernity and a modernity that is attentive to liturgy that lives and moves us does not have to be considered a sin any longer, if I have read correctly even the most recent magisterial liturgical documents.

In this way, at the cost of this audacity and patience, we all can truly *receive the liturgical movement as entrusted to us by the liturgical reform, by responding carefully and effectively to the liturgical question, a question that was not closed by* Mediator Dei, *Vatican II, or the liturgical reform. Nor will it be closed by us or by the generation of Catholics that follow us.* This makes the liturgical movement the greatest and most important outcome of the liturgical reform: a liturgical movement in its third phase, the most delicate phase precisely because it is the least clear, the most decisive, and so also the most fragile.

Kierkegaard was right. There are things that every generation must begin again from the start. Yet in a true multigenerational work like the *liturgia reformanda*, every single generation must work hard to avoid both the despair of impotence and the presumption of omnipotence. It must do only that which it can, with great patience, but fully and profoundly, with great courage. This is the necessary "militance" to which I alluded earlier: to bear the tension between unsurpassed courage and patience, which ennobles and characterizes the theological work on the liturgy, yesterday's as well as today's and tomorrow's.

Only in this way can every generation—even ours—hope to remain truly within the tradition of the *ecclesia Christi*, allowing future generations also truly and fully to drink of it, with the *bitterness* that hardens hearts and strains bodies and with all the *sweetness* that brings comfort and consolation to men and women, to the hopes of the old and the uncertainties of the children, to the thoughts of the wise and the dreams of fools.

Of such an *ecclesia* the liturgy can be truly *culmen* only if it is truly *fons*. This is the open wound of the liturgical question: it falls within the context of the liturgical reform but is also beyond the liturgical reform, before its necessity and beyond its insufficiency. But it is only here that the liturgists of both today and tomorrow can find their specific field of work, at the service

of the church, certainly, but with all the courage possible and not without all the patience necessary.

Chapter 5

Liturgical Reform and Virtual Reality

Benedict XVI's Motu Proprio *Summorum Pontificum* and the Ecclesia Dei Commission's Instruction *Universae Ecclesiae*

> The most important principles governing a general liturgical reform should be laid before the members of the hierarchy at the forthcoming ecumenical council.
>
> —John XXIII
> *Rubricarum instructum*[1]

Just a few months after the first edition of this volume was published, Pope Benedict XVI's motu proprio *Summorum Pontificum* was promulgated on July 7, 2007, accompanied by his Letter to the Bishops on the Use of the Roman Liturgy Prior to the Reform of 1970. The reader, approaching the text with great respect, is immediately struck by an acute sense of disorientation and a certain confusion, to the point of wondering: What century am I in, and in what church? What liturgy and what Mass are we talking about?

---

[1] John XXIII, Apostolic Letter Motu Proprio *Rubricarum Instructum*, July 25, 1960.

The cause of this understandable reaction is found in the notable courage—or, perhaps more accurately, in the audacity—with which Benedict XVI chose to confront the thorny question of the unity of the church in light of the conflict of interpretations of the liturgical reform. His strategy consisted of a rereading of the history of the last century that, while presented in a profoundly classic style, offers an approach of such novelty that it leaves the reader utterly amazed and confused. One has the sense of being confronted by an authoritative *virtual reality*, one aimed decisively at overcoming ecclesial conflicts but that has a complex and problematic impact on *real reality* in its daily concreteness and mundane opacity. And this should be noted in order to avoid what Cardinal Camillo Ruini called, in his enthusiastic comments about the document, "the risk that a motu proprio whose intention is to unite the Christian community might instead be used to divide it."[2]

In order to offer a careful interpretation of the document and its possible pastoral effects, I would first like to briefly summarize its contents and intentions and then to evaluate, with critical respect and in a loyal dialogue of communion, the impact on real reality that such a normative version of a virtual reality might hold for the future of the church and its liturgy.

1. THE MOTU PROPRIO *SUMMORUM PONTIFICUM*: TWO FORMS OF THE SAME RITE
The text of *Summorum Pontificum* opens with a long historical preface. Moving from Gregory the Great through John Paul II, it summarizes the development of the Roman Rite, noting the decisive impact of the work

---

[2] C. Ruini, Editorial in *Avvenire*, July 8, 2007, p.1.

of Saint Pius V, promoter of the Roman Missal, which "with the passing of the centuries, little by little took forms very similar to that it has had in recent times."[3] The pope then comes to the reform mandated by the Second Vatican Council and the reformed Missal of Pope Paul VI, which, having been translated into most of the languages of the world, was well received by bishops, priests, and faithful alike. And yet, Benedict recalls, John Paul II found it necessary in 1984 and again in 1988 to concede to "no small numbers of faithful" the indult to use the "the earlier liturgical forms [which] had so deeply marked their culture and their spirit."

From this historical consideration, *Summorum Pontificum* now offers a new ruling on the issue. Reiterating that the Missal of Paul VI remains "the ordinary expression of the *lex orandi* of the Catholic Church of the Latin rite," Benedict affirms that the Tridentine missal, in the edition of John XXIII of 1962, must be considered the "extraordinary expression of the same *lex orandi*" (no. 1). *There are, therefore, two uses of the same* lex orandi *common to Pius V and Paul VI.* From here, Benedict rules that "it is, therefore, permissible to celebrate the Sacrifice of the Mass following the typical edition of the Roman Missal promulgated by Bl. John XXIII in 1962 and never abrogated."

[3] [The quotations included here are from the unofficial English translation of *Summorum Pontificum* provided by the Vatican Information Service, available in an appendix of Marc Aillet, *The Old Mass and the New: Explaining the Motu Proprio* Summorum Pontificum *of Pope Benedict XVI* (San Francisco: Ignatius, 2010), 97–103, and at http:// www.ewtn.com/library/papaldoc/b16summorum pontificum.htm. On the Vatican web site, *Summorum Pontificum* is available—as of June 2013—only in Latin and, curiously, Hungarian. —Trans.]

The conditions for its celebration are spelled out in *Summorum Pontificum* in the eleven articles that follow. In Masses celebrated "without the people," there is full parallelism of the two "uses," except for the paschal Triduum (no. 2). This possibility is also extended to conventual Masses, with the approval of the major superiors (no. 3). Specifying that any of the faithful who wish it must be admitted to the above-mentioned Masses without the people (no. 4), the document spells out the discipline for Masses with the people, where a group of the faithful "who adhere to the earlier liturgical tradition" can have daily Mass, Mass on Sundays and feast days, and Masses on the occasion of matrimony, funerals, and pilgrimages celebrated according to the extraordinary form (no. 5). The readings in these cases can be in the vernacular (no. 6). If the priest does not respond to these requests, the bishop can do so or refer the matter to the Ecclesia Dei Commission in order to receive counsel or help (nos. 7–8). Priests are also granted the faculties to celebrate baptism, matrimony, penance, and anointing of the sick according to the extraordinary use; the ordinary of a diocese can celebrate confirmation according to the previous Roman Pontifical; and clerics can use the Roman Breviary of 1962 (no. 9). Finally, the erection of personal parishes are envisioned to ensure the celebration according to the Tridentine use (no. 10), and the new compentencies of the Ecclesia Dei Commission, to keep watch over the application of all of these elements, are defined (nos. 11–12).

2. THE LETTER TO THE BISHOPS: THE LITURGICAL REFORM IS NOT WEAKENED

The letter that Pope Benedict XVI addressed to the world's bishops on the occasion of the publication of the motu proprio has three important and central themes. The first two address the "fears" that had become manifest in the months leading up to the publication of *Summorum Pontificum* and that the Bishop of Rome wanted to clarify for his brother bishops.

First of all, the letter denies that the authority of the Second Vatican Council is weakened by *Summorum Pontificum*, since it reaffirms that the ordinary and normal form of the Roman Missal remains the one promulgated by Paul VI. The letter recounts the history of the presence of the preceding Ordo alongside the Novus Ordo up to these new norms, which remedy an issue "which had not been foreseen at the time of the 1988 Motu Proprio." It concludes by saying, "The present norms are also meant to free Bishops from constantly having to evaluate anew how they are to respond to various situations."

The second fear is that of those who hypothesize that this parallelism of ritual forms "would lead to disarray or even divisions within parish communities." That possibility is excluded by the fact that the use of the preconciliar Missal "presupposes a certain degree of liturgical formation and some knowledge of the Latin language; neither of these is found very often." The letter points instead to the "mutual enrichment" of the two ritual forms.

Finally, in its third point, the letter to the bishops offers the "positive reason" that has motivated Benedict XVI in this new ruling: "It is a matter of coming to an interior reconciliation in the heart of the Church," wishing to make every possible effort to guarantee unity. Then comes the judgment that *Summorum Pontificum* has made normative: "There is no contradiction between the two editions of the Roman Missal. In the history of the liturgy there is growth and progress, but no rupture. What earlier generations held as sacred, remains sacred and great for us too, and it cannot be all of a sudden entirely forbidden or even considered harmful." This calls also for a necessary reciprocity: "the priests of the communities adhering to the former usage cannot, as a matter of principle, exclude celebrating according to the new books."

In conclusion, the letter calls for the bishops, three years after the promulgation of *Summorum Pontificum*, to inform the Holy See of their experiences and of any difficulties that come to light.

3. CRITICAL REFLECTION: THE DIFFERENCE BETWEEN INTENTIONS AND EFFECTS, BETWEEN VIRTUAL AND REAL

Having considered the contents of *Summorum Pontificum* and the letter to the bishops, we can now better evaluate its intentions and effects. Naturally, in this regard, a theologian's role is to use the *intellectus fidei* not only to repeat or to applaud but also to carry out the ecclesial service that is specific to theological work and that is essential to the church's thoughtful discernment and critical reception. On the basis of this "ecclesial vocation of the theologian"—which must always be exercised with audacity and patience, humility and courage—I think five important questions must be considered, each of which merit calm evaluation and urgent ecclesial reflection.

The Juridical Question: Which Rite Is in Force?

Saint Thomas Aquinas wrote with great insight, "If we resolve the questions related to the faith simply by means of authority, we will certainly possess the truth, but in empty heads."[4] We should keep this pre-Tridentine admonition in mind as we evaluate the post-Tridentine affirmations of Pope Benedict's motu proprio. *Summorum Pontificum* argues—twice—that "the rite of Pius V was never abrograted." The statement sounds obvious, barely worth mentioning, if not that it comes from the pope himself. But that does not prevent our heads, if we don't want them to be empty, from taking note of a series of other affirmations, each uncontested and completely valid. Canon 20 of the Code of Canon Law, a famous 1999 Response of the Congregation for Divine Worship,[5] and the traditional wisdom of Cardinal Giuseppe Siri[6] each insist that the approval of a new liturgical rite (of the Eucharist as with every other liturgy) means that the preceding rite is *de facto*

[4] St. Thomas Aquinas, *Quodlibet* 4, q. 9, a. 3, corpus. "Si nudis auctoritatibus magister questionem determinet, certificabitur quidem auditor quod ita est, sed nihil scientiae vel intellectus acquiret et vacuus abscedet."

[5] Canon 20 of the *Codex Juris Canonici* reads: "Lex posterior abrogat priorem aut eidem derogat, si id expresse edicat aut illi sit directe contraria, aut totam de integro ordinet legis prioris materiam." Consistent with this principle, the Response of the Congregation for Divine Worship of July 3, 1999 (prot. 1411/99), says explicitly: "The Roman Missal approved and promulgated by the authority of Pope Paul VI . . . *is the only form of celebration of the Holy Sacrifice according to the Roman Rite currently in force, in consonance with the single general liturgical law.*"

[6] Twenty-five years ago, when an English monk wrote to Cardinal Siri of Genoa, asking him the most appropriate approach to liturgical matters in the case of doubt between the old and the new rite, the cardinal responded: "The power with which Pius V instituted his liturgical reform is the same power that Paul VI used. The presence of the reformed Ordo implies its substitution for the older one" (letter of 6 September 1982).

replaced by the new one. Just as there is a fundamental need for "certainty of law," so there is also a need for "certainty of rite."

This being the case, it is not necessary for anyone to demonstate that the Missal of Paul VI abrograted the missal that was in force from 1962 to 1969, because this is clear according to common liturgical law. It is up to those who would argue otherwise to provide the proof to support it. As long as they do not offer reasonable arguments of a juridical or liturgical nature, as long as the "double contemporary form" is only affirmed, but not demonstrated and proven, the general principle may be presumed: the newer Roman Rite substitutes the older Roman Rite, and a conflict cannot replace the simple fact that only one rite, only one form, and only one use is in force, according to the principle of common law (not to mention common sense).

To that we can add, to be thorough, another consideration. Not only is it impossible to deduce from the text of *Sacrosanctum Concilium* some parallel existence of two ritual forms in force in the single Roman Rite;[7] in fact, such an idea clearly runs contrary to the conciliar text, which indicates clear intentions of revision and substitution of the preconciliar liturgy.[8] Indeed,

[7] One can reach such conclusions only by the most forced and implausible readings, bringing the reader not only to the edge of dismay but even beyond the limits of good taste. Cf., for example, the *Dossier*, edited by N. Bux and A. Vitiello, *Il Motu Proprio di Benedetto XVI "Summorum Pontificum cura,"* of the FIDES Agency, dated 1 August 2007, available on the internet at www.fides.va.

[8] For example, consider the wording of SC 25 and 128: "The liturgical books are to be revised as soon as possible; experts are to be employed on the task, and bishops are to be consulted, from various parts of the world" (SC 25); "Along with the revision of

a great many implementing measures of the reform, promulgated by Pope Paul VI, demonstrate a clear intention to substitute the older ritual regime with the newer one (as has been the case throughout the history of the church). Furthermore, one can even recognize such an intention in Paul's predecessor, John XXIII, who, in the document that introduces and makes possible the 1962 edition of the Tridentine missal, emphasizes not only the desire to continue (and bring to completion) Pope Pius XII's project of a complete revision of the rubrics of the Breviary and of the Roman Missal but of doing so for the period of time—still difficult to foresee in 1960—until the convocation of the Second Vatican Council and the work of liturgical reform that it was expected to accomplish.[9] It should not

---

the liturgical books, as laid down in Art. 25, there is to be an early revision of the canons and ecclesiastical statutes which govern the provision of material things involved in sacred worship. These laws refer especially to the worthy and well planned construction of sacred buildings, the shape and construction of altars. . . . *Laws which seem less suited to the reformed liturgy are to be brought into harmony with it, or else abolished; and any which are helpful are to be retained if already in use, or introduced where they are lacking"* (SC 128, italics mine). The *mens* of the Council should be noted: there is no reference to "parallel traditions," but there is explicit reference to "corrections," "abolition," well beyond "new introductions." On the other hand, the weakness of the theory of the "parallel usage" becomes clear when one considers today the need for "adjustment" of the liturgical space, explicitly desired by the Council, and that a theory of "parallel ritual forms" would render not only difficult in fact but even impossible in principle.

[9] The document in question is John XXIII's Motu Proprio *Rubricarum Instructum* (July 25, 1960), with which he carries on the project of Pius XII. While developing the plan and the preparatory studies for a general liturgical reform, he decided first to revise the

surprise us, then, that the Missal of 1962—the very one that is today claimed to have force *sine die* alongside the one approved by Pope Paul VI—was approved by Pope John XXIII as a "provisional text" in expectation

---

rubrics of the Roman Breviary but then, after having consulted the bishops, took up the project of complex revision of the rubrics of the Breviary and the Roman Missal, entrusting this work to the commission in charge of the general reform of the liturgy. In doing so, John XXIII added: "*Nos autem, postquam, adspirante Deo, Concilium Oecumenicum coadunandum esse decrevimus, quid circa huiusmodi Predecessoris Nostri inceptum agendum foret, haud semel recogitavimus. Re itaque diu ac mature examinata, in sententiam devenimus, altiora principia, generalem liturgicam instaurationem respicentia, in proximo Concilio Oecumenico patribus esse proponenda; memoratam vero rubricarum Breviarii ac Messalis emendationem diutius non esse protrahendam.*" ["After we had decided, under the inspiration of God, to convene an ecumenical council, we turned over in our mind what was to be done about this project begun by our predecessor. After mature reflection, we came to the conclusion that the more important principles governing a general liturgical reform should be laid before the members of the hierarchy at the forthcoming ecumenical council, but that the above-mentioned improvement of the rubrics of the breviary and missal should no longer be put off." Translation in R. Kevin Seasoltz, *The New Liturgy: A Documentation, 1903–1965* (New York: Herder & Herder, 1966), 305. —Trans.] Evident here is the tension created by the project of the imminent Council between the limited revision of the rubrics and the rethinking of the "altiora principia" that led to the more general reform of the Roman Rite. The edition of the Roman Missal that was published two years later was intended for use during the "interregnum" between the rite of Pius V and the one that would eventually be produced by the liturgical reform (by Paul VI). It was, in short, a provisional revision, but one that could not be postponed, of the preceding rubrical system, in view of a more complex rethinking that would come, the need for which was already recognized in 1962 but which the Pope could not anticipate by "motu proprio," precisely because of the solemn celebration of the Council that was to come.

of the Council and of the liturgical reform that was in 1960 already expected to result from it.

The nonabrogation of the Missal of Pius V, then, means little. Supporting such a central and decisive affirmation with an argument from silence—together with the fact that two preceding popes (one could even say three, since, as we have seen, one could also include John XXIII) each understood the postconciliar rite as the only one effectively in force, making exception to this case by the use of indult—raises an objective and urgent problem that must be clarified in some other way, in order not to leave a grave uncertainty that would certainly influence reasoning and practice on related matters.

By authority, one obeys, but reason wishes for something more, which is now sought in vain. To cite Augustine: "To learn, two guides are necessary: authority and reason. In the order of time authority comes first, while in the order of the nature of things, reason is first."[10]

The Theological Question:
What Is the Relevance of the Lex Orandi?

Lex orandi statuat legem credendi. ("The norm of the liturgy establishes the norm of the church's faith.") This famous expression by Prosper of Aquitain serves as the foundation of the most important article of *Summorum Pontificum* (no. 1). It is one of the principles of the liturgical movement, establishing the fundamental place of the liturgical action in the act of faith. But *Summorum Pontificum* proposes an understanding of the statement that introduces a distinction that is both

---

[10] Augustine, *De Ordine*, 2.26.

original and quite consequential. According to the document, the relationship between *lex orandi* and *lex credendi* is preceded by the relationship between the different ritual uses (or expressions, or forms) and a single *lex orandi*. This means that here the notion of *lex orandi* is identified not with a rite but with the meaning, the content of the rite. Introducing this distinction, *Summorum Pontificum* does two things at the same time: it creates a space for bringing together two different uses, reconciling them in a single *lex orandi* and avoiding two different *leges orandi* giving life to two different professions of faith; at the same time, it also distances the *lex orandi* from the ritual concreteness that distinguishes it.

If *"lex orandi"* no longer means the rite as it is concretely celebrated, a specific "ordo," but instead refers to an existential, invisible, and/or conceptual dimension, then the rite tends to shift fundamentally and irretrievably into a secondary position with respect to the faith. One who lacks the liturgical sensibility of Benedict XVI might even read this distinction as the essential subordination of the liturgical celebration to purely dogmatic facts, of which the two "uses" would constitute merely practical translations of the dogma that have no role in determining it. In other words, accepting the idea of the single *lex orandi* in two alternative "forms" would restore the primacy of theology over liturgy, giving up one of the most conspicuous achievements of the liturgical movement.

Furthermore, if we insist that there is now a single rite with two different "uses," how can we ever speak historically of two different "ordines"? Is the ordo only a "use" of a rite, or is it the rite itself? And does a difference of *ordines* mean ritual difference of *lex orandi*, or does it not? To answer these questions, we have to consider the relationship of *Summorum Pontificum* with certain affirmations of Pope Benedict's postsynodal apostolic exhortation *Sacramentum Caritatis*. What theology of the sacraments can be developed from the "celebration"—given the "primacy of the *liturgical action*" referred to in paragraph 34 of that document—if different actions change neither the *lex orandi* nor the *lex credendi*?[11]

Second, we must ask if the same distinction between ordinary use and extraordinary use constitutes a distinction of fact or of law. On this point—which, as we have already seen, is theoretically decisive—rests some real perplexity, having to do with both the distinction as such and the effective comparability of the two different "uses." In the first place, it is not clear whether the distiction between ordinary and extraordinary use is *de facto* or *de iure*. If it is *de facto*, it would lack authentic normative force, while if it is *de iure*, it would find all its authority confirmed. But one could deduce from the tenor of the text—certainly with considerable interpretation, but it would be possible—that that which is in fact ordinary must become extraordinary, while that which is in fact extraordinary must *de iure* be understood as ordinary. There does not seem to be a true pedagogy of the ordinary with regard to the

---

[11] To offer a single example: If beginning Mass "without the people" or "when the people are gathered" is indifferent for eucharistic theology, that means, in essence, that the liturgical action has nothing to say to sacramental theology and that theology is substantially autonomous of the liturgy. The same observation could be made in the case of any substantial variation between the preconciliar and postconciliar rites.

extraordinary. The absence of local episcopal control regarding the relationship between the two different uses also suggests that its *de iure* nature is not sufficiently clear, risking a crisis of ordinary pastoral ministry, where the local bishop lacks control over the liturgy and when there is no *de iure* situation that is clearly binding upon all.[12]

Third, the consequences of treating two "forms" equally, the most recent of which is the fruit of the careful reform of the previous, remain unclear. In other words, it is difficult to see how the liberalization of the older rite would not arouse a grave tension in those who practice the newer rite, who would justifiably understand the Tridentine Rite as having been "superceded," "reformed," and "emended" by the succeeding rite. The two "uses" are not autonomous: one is the response to a crisis of the other. Therefore, one cannot avoid feeling a grave uneasiness at the reappearance of the old form, as though nothing had happened. Furthermore, the introduction of the two parallel "uses" alongside each other, presented as an "adding without detracting," in reality introduces an element of disparity between a "structurally plural" use, like that of Paul VI (which is presented in a variety of languages and of adaptations that are constitutive of it) and the

---

[12] Confusing the matter even more is the very structure of the document *Summorum Pontificum*. *On the level of content,* the rite of Paul VI is called "ordinary," while that of Pius V is "extraordinary." But *on the level of form,* the document adopts the extraordinary categories of Pius V (distinguishing between a private Mass and Mass with the people) and not those of Paul VI (which speaks only of "participated Mass"). The embarrassment that results seems justified.

monolithic univocity of the Tridentine Rite (which can be offered only in Latin and without any adaptations).

The Pastoral Question: Does It Guarantee Ecclesial Communion and/or Freedom of Rite?

In 2001, at a conference organized by the Abbey of Fontgombault, Joseph Ratzinger, then the cardinal prefect of the Congregation for the Doctrine of the Faith, argued that the desirable broader use of the Tridentine Rite must be tempered by the episcopal guarantee of liturgical unity in a diocese.[13] *Summorum Pontificum* rejects the logic of the 1984 and 1988 indults, which attribute to local episcopal authority the possibility of granting the necessary authorization for making exception to a clear rule. This logic rested on the understanding that only one rite was in force, while another rite had a limited, problematic, and conditional practicability, so that it could be celebrated by exception to its normal status as a "rite no longer in force."

Modifying this logic, substituting it with the parallelism of two "uses" (or forms) of the same rite, raises these questions: How can the bishops ensure ecclesial communion on the liturgical level, discerning between the ordinary use and the extraordinary use? How can they prevent the rise of a divisive bi-ritualism and the introduction of divisions, disagreements, and misunderstandings in the ecclesial body, not only in the area

---

[13] Cf. *Autour de la question liturgique. Avec le Cardinal Ratzinger,* Actes des Journées liturgiques de Fontgombault 22–24 Juillet 2001, Association Petrus a Stella (Fontgombault, 2001). [ET: Alcuin Reid, ed., *Looking again at the Question of the Liturgy with Cardinal Ratzinger: Proceedings of the July 2001 Fontgombault Liturgical Conference* (St Michaels Abbey, 2004). —Trans.]

of liturgy, but also in catechesis, formation, evangelization, and charity? The wording of the document remains vague, even indifferent, on this topic, even attributing a competence to the Ecclesia Dei Commission that nullifies the ordinary competence of the Congregation for Divine Worship, despite the fact that the recent history of the former offers no reason to think that it might approach these matters in an impartial way. If, to confirm this, we read the brief but authoritative preface that Ecclesia Dei president Cardinal Castrillon Hojos wrote recently for the new edition of the Trimeloni liturgical manual, we are left troubled by the utter lack of a sense of history that it reveals—though we might be reassured by Hoyos's notable sense of humor.

The Liturgical Question: A Necessary Reform or an Accessory Reform?

In interview comments offered by supporters at the time of *Summorum Pontificum*'s release, as well as in the pope's accompanying letter to bishops, we are told repeatedly that there is no intention to criticize the liturgical reform that followed Vatican II. And there is no reason to doubt this, at least in terms of the fundamental intentions of the document and its author. With regard to its objective effects, however, no one can deny that the publication of *Summorum Pontificum* raises the risk of radically relativizing the meaning and the historical significance of the reform.

In the perspective of the document, the reform would no longer be understood as the norm of our celebration, formation, spirituality, and edification; it would instead be only an addendum—albeit a distinguished one—to a preceding tradition, which would be restored intact, with all its rites and its calendar, as if nothing had happened, turning back the ecclesial clocks to 1962. The church would have to live, at the same time, in the twenty-first century and in 1962, subordinating the choice not to the discretion of the bishop but to the decision of the faithful and/or to the "free" choice of individual priests. The liturgical reform, which aimed at reforming the Roman Tridentine Rite to promote active participation, would end up reduced to an option, unable to influence the "ancient" and "high" tradition of the Mass, which would become therefore "irreformable."

All of this would constitute, in effect, a reductive rereading and a caricature of the intentions of the Council. It would run the risk of forgetting *Sacrosanctum Concilium*'s call (nos. 47–57) to rediscover in the Eucharist the richness of Scripture, the homily, the prayer of the faithful, the vernacular, the unity of the two tables, Communion under both forms, and concelebration. We must recall—and it should perhaps be included in another letter, to be posted on the doors of every sacristy—that not a single one of these seven elements is found in the Tridentine Rite, that the reform was necessary to make them reality, and that only by means of the reform did the Roman Rite rediscover its lost riches. Is the "freedom" we seek the freedom to return to a scriptural poverty, a homiletic poverty, a poverty of the prayer of the faithful, a poverty of the vernacular language, a poverty of Communion under both forms, and a poverty of concelebration?[14] How could

---

[14] For a well-grounded reflection on the richness of the new Ordo compared to the poverty of the preceding one, cf. Patrick Regan, *Advent to Pentecost: Comparing the Seasons in the Ordinary and Extra-*

the church deprive itself of these riches without losing much of its capacity for witness? And why should the law, in this case, be understood simply as "legislation of what is possible" rather than invoking its pedagogical and formative power, which in so many other cases is emphasized strongly?

The Practical Question: Who Will Be Able to Celebrate the Preconciliar Rite?

Chesterton said, "When Christians enter a church, they remove their hats, not their heads." And keeping one's head on one's shoulders—that is, common sense—means not letting our desires push us too far into abstraction or imagination. It might be easy to convince ourselves, simply by speaking of "another rite," that such a thing exists and that it is available and manageable, *semper et ubique,* by anyone. In reality—if one dares to face reality—it is not so and can never be so.

One can preside or assist at the preconciliar rite only if one has been adequately formed to do so, as Benedict's Letter to the Bishops notes clearly. The radical difficulty of this is written irreversibly into the history of the church of the last fifty years. For fifty years, we have formed Christians, including priests—at least in 95 percent of dioceses—according to the languages, the cultures, the theologies, and the spiritualities that are written into the gestures and the silences, the texts and the styles, the rites and the songs of the new liturgy. That is so true for our minds and rooted so deeply in our bodies that most parish priests, if approached by their parishioners with a request for a Mass celebrated

---

ordinary Forms of the Roman Rite (Collegeville, MN: Liturgical Press, 2012).

according to the rite of Pius V, could in honesty only respond, "I'm sorry, but I can't. It is neither the church nor the liturgy in which I learned to believe, to live, and to pray." Each of us formed after the Second Vatican Council—and we now make up the great majority of the church—is *beyond* the Mass of Pius V. Like it or not, we cannot go backward. In the ordinary pastoral work of the great majority of dioceses, the celebration of some "ancient use" is neither practical nor realistic.

4. A PRELIMINARY ASSESSMENT, OPEN AND HEARTFELT

In a 2007 article supportive of the restoration of the "Tridentine Mass,"[15] René Girard wrote that "unity brings conflict, pluralism brings peace."[16] Benedict XVI would call this is "relativism." But don't we find a similar argument in *Summorum Pontificum*? Isn't it, rather, unity that guarantees communion, while plurality can fracture, tempting everyone to believe themselves to be part of the one and "true" church? And couldn't this traditionalist shift with regard to liturgical matters be understood as incredibly liberal and secularized in its language and thought? Couldn't this "free choice" in liturgy be understood as *indifference* toward the liturgy and as promoting a sort of *Christian gnosticism*?

[15] R. Girard, *La Repubblica*, July 3, 2007, p. 34.

[16] Girard's paradoxical reading of the papal action culminates in this thought: "Making absolute rules guarantees conflict. If on the other hand rigid norms are not imposed, there will be no conflicts because there will be no disagreements: no one will have a problem. The Mass is one of those matters that can never be the object of administrative regulation!" Clearly, these conclusions do not quite represent the thinking of Benedict XVI.

This certainly is not Benedict's intention, but it is true in terms of *Summorum Pontificum*'s objective and indisputable dissonance with the liturgical reform. Therefore, theology, respectfully critical and critically respectful, cannot fail to raise legitimate and loyal objections, so that the communion of the church might not suffer a grave liturgical *vulnus* and that the liturgy can continue to be *culmen et fons* and not merely a variable and negotiable explication of the *lex credendi*.

For all of these reasons, it seems to me that the noble intentions of protecting peace and concord in Catholic liturgy have been used to justify the use of instruments so modern and bold that they threaten to gravely undermine the history of the last fifty years of the liturgical movement. In effect, we can agree that the liturgical movement did not end with the Second Vatican Council and the reform and that it must continue on after these events, because ours is a tradition that includes not only an important past that must be defended but also the irreplaceable richness of a complex present and a wide-open future: "The persistence of a liturgy that is considered immutable can certainly satisfy the strong psycho-religious desire for continuity, but it can never realize the need to seize 'the hour of grace.'"[17] The "organic development" of liturgical tradition inevitably brings "shifts," with a continuity that must include some vital discontinuity. As is the case in the passing of generations—where the child is fully a son only when the father is no longer there at his side—a rite of Paul VI that always has the rite of Pius V at its side will remain perpetually childish

[17] A. Angenendt, *Liturgia e storia. Lo sviluppo organico in questione* (Assisi: Cittadella, 2005), 239.

and fragile, and a rite of Pius V that is not permitted to disappear into its child would fall into an intrusive paternalism and moralism that lacks trust. Without ever clearly expressing the intention of denying this providential detachment, *Summorum Pontificum* lends itself too easily to such an interpretation, precisely in this gap between virtual reality and real reality. It offers support to an understanding of tradition that is static, not dynamic; monumental and archeological, not vital; where nothing is lost, everything accumulates, but nothing is alive anymore.[18] For this reason, to avoid such readings, it is good to recall Blondel's comment, a century ago, in defense of the dynamism that is constitutive of tradition: "It is not the idea of development, which worries so many believers, that is heterodox; rather, it is fixism . . . that is virtually a heresy."[19] By distinguishing between the *lex orandi* and "uses" of the same *lex*, the motu proprio opens itself to the same criticism, and some will inevitably put its words to their own uses. Can we expect even for *Summorum Pontificum* an "extraordinary use" of its words for highly traditionalistic purposes?

[18] In this, A. Gerhards saw the danger in a distorted reading of history: "What disturbs me above all is the distorted representation of the liturgical renewal of the twentieth century. It is presented as though some experts sitting around a table destroyed a rite that came directly from the Holy Spirit to Gregory the Great in the sixth century. . . . Large parts of the Order of Mass of 1570 developed only around 1500" (A. Gerhards, "'Come se la riforma fosse stata un incidente'" (interview with Albert Gerhards by J. Franck), *Kölner Stadt-Anzeiger*, July 6, 2007 (http://rhein-sieg-anzeiger.ksta .de/html/artikel/1182933878509.shtml).

[19] M. Blondel, *Storia e dogma. Le lacune filosofiche dell'esegesi moderna* (Brescia: Queriniana, 1992), 119.

God forbid that a bold conception of a virtual reality, like that offered by *Summorum Pontificum*, might offer objective and implicit support—and almost an excess of authority—not to real efforts to bring peace to the church, but to a "virtual heresy."

5. *UNIVERSAE* OR *INTROVERSAE ECCLESIAE*?

Prophetically, the day after the publication of *Summorum Pontificum* in July 2007, Cardinal Ruini recognized "the risk that a motu proprio whose intention is to unite the Christian community might instead be used to divide it." In the wake of *Summorum Pontificum* and the Letter to Bishops that accompanied it, this recent instruction seems to have confirmed Cardinal Ruini's prophecy decisively: the division that had been a real possibility is now an easily recognized reality.

It has to be said: the effort showed signs of problems right from the start. When a rereading of a ritual tradition is proposed that reanimates a rite no longer in force, presuming facts that are untrue and creating juridical fictions that lack grounding in reality—conceiving, in a daring balancing act, a situation of two different forms existing in force in a parallel way, living together in the same Roman Rite—the knot of contradictions can only get tighter. No matter how many committees are set up, how many consultations occur, how many DVDs of the preconciliar Mass are produced and distributed, how many "rights of the faithful" are recognized, the confusion only increases and the bewilderment does not go away.

Now this most recent link in the chain—the instruction *Universae Ecclesiae*[20] —is burdened by a structurally insoluble problem: how do you "teach" a glaring contradiction? The more it is taught, the less is understood. If all of the sudden, with the support of yet-unknown principles of law and tradition, a rite that was no longer in force, having been replaced by a reformed version of itself, is magically restored to being in force—notwithstanding anything established or contemplated by Pope Paul VI, Pope John XXIII, or the Code of Canon Law—and purports to apply in a parallel way to the rite that had amended, renewed, and replaced it, then everything undergoes a sort of unavoidable deformation. When attachments and nostalgia are treated as principles of ecclesial order, there are bound to be problems. In fact, according to the logic of this highly problematic vision, any priest might now choose to celebrate any ritual form of the Eucharist they prefer, as long as they do it "in private." Truly instructive: two individualistic contradictions, overlapping one another, achieve nothing more than a paradoxical form of noncelebration and nonidentity.

On the other hand, with regard to the faithful, any group might claim the right to have a Mass celebrated according to a rite no longer in force. With all the precision of a multiplex-cinema ecclesiology, the instruction's conception of a "group of the faithful" might be comprised of one lay person from Bergamo, one from Vicenza, three from Como (but from different parishes,

[20] [Pontifical Commission Ecclesia Dei, *Instruction on the Application of the Apostolic Letter* Summorum Pontificum *of His Holiness Benedict XVI Given* Motu Proprio, April 30, 2011. —Trans.]

of course), and one from Novara. Even this is truly very instructive of the communal nature of the church.

But there is more. The logic of the extraordinary rite is so exceptional that, when it clashes with reality, it has the strength to bend even the law. And so when the existing Code of Canon Law does not correspond with the rubrics of the rite no longer in force, no problem: the law that was in force in 1962 must be applied, the Code of 1917, despite being no longer in force today. There is nothing to fear: it is simply that the rite no longer in force corresponds to the law no longer in force. What is more instructive than this?

And again, even if ordination is not ordinarily conferred in the extraordinary rite, still in certain cases exceptions can be made, and the faculty for ordaining according to the preconciliar rite is given. How can this pointed clarification of possible exception to the supposedly sacrosanct untouchability of the ordination rite not be seen as instructive?

Then there is the question of which priests are deemed "suitable" to celebrate according to the rite that is no longer in force. It is true that they have to deal with the Latin language, but familiarizing themselves with the five declensions and having some experience of the verb forms are sufficient requisites. And then, regarding adequate knowledge of the execution of the rite, priests who present themselves "spontaneously" are presumed to be qualified. The instructive effect here borders on a subtle and smug irony.

The many details of the new instruction—of which we have cited only a few remarkable examples—illustrate well the inexorable chain of paradoxes into which we stumble when we lose a sense of reality and follow the way of a dream, of illusion, right into the danger of mystification. What can be said about the fact that we will now insert into the 1962 Missal new saints and new prefaces? What are we to think of now reforming a rite that has already been reformed, complete with the new saints, new prefaces, new collects, new biblical readings, new eucharistic prayers, new super oblatas, new postcommunion prayers? Now we need another reform, adding saints and prefaces to the 1962 rite? But are we now in 2013? Have we perhaps just awoken, after a half-century dream? How can we not consider all of this dancing in midair to be nothing more than a waste of energy and strength?

All things considered, it is hard to deny that the 1962 rite fell out of force from the moment Pope Paul VI approved the new form of the Roman Rite. From this point of view, the Roman Rite is made alive and thriving for the tradition by the new form, while the 1962 form—defined as provisional by explicit declaration of Pope John XXIII—is replaced. Every attempt, no matter how authoritative, to deny this evidence will inevitably result only in illusions, contradictions, and confusion.

The intent of the motu proprio was to restore communion lost by the Lefebvrian schism. Now with several years' distance, and with all that has happened since 2007, this objective appears to be still quite far off, which is not to say unattainable. The instruction says, rather, that the motu proprio "has made the richness of the Roman Liturgy more accessible to the Universal Church." This statement attempts to disconnect *Summorum Pontificum* from the contingent justification that originally motivated it. It is an instruction that is intended to resolve problems but truly resolves nothing—certainly not theologically—and here, unfortunately, my opinion is that it attemps to do theology with too little effort.

Conclusion

> I would like to make only two brief points: (1) The liturgy is a *living* thing, but *fragile*; in the hands of one who does not know how to handle it, it dies. (2) The liturgy is a *living* thing, but only if it is *dynamic*, facing always toward the future, with the proviso that its dynamism lives between two poles: that of the mystery of salvation *realized* by Christ and that of the same mystery of salvation which *must be realized* in us.[1]

The achievements of the liturgical movement are too precious to risk being lost or forgotten. And the words with which I open this conclusion seem to express well what the "liturgical question" is all about, to which the liturgical reform has offered an initial, but not final, response. That the liturgy is at the same time both living and fragile, living and dynamic, is a truth that is hard to bear but one that is crucial for Christian living.

Every project of liturgical traditionalism conceives the liturgy only *in its absolute fragility*, without some attention to its *necessary dynamism*. It is, at most, a fresco that must be cleaned and restored, nothing more. Vice versa, every project of liturgical progressivism sees the liturgy only in its *dynamic growth*, forgetting its *great*

---

[1] S. Marsili, "*Rivista Liturgica* 1914–1974: 60 anni di servizio al Movimento Liturgico," *Rivista Liturgica* 61 (1974): 22–34, here 34; cited in P. Visentin's farewell to the journal, *Rivista Liturgica* 83 (1996): 629.

fragility, with all the care, wisdom, and dexerity that demands.

But one cannot restore the "true liturgy" solely on the basis of history, taking refuge in outdated rituals and forgetting the dynamism of cultures and the always changing forms of life, historical experiences, and symbolic expressions. A merely nostalgic response to the liturgical question on the part of the church was rejected more than a century ago. Today it remains an option only for those tiny minorities that, then as now, make nostalgia their identity and presumption their only hope.

The most authentic way to resist these temptations—which are too often evident and even dominant in the great body of the church—is to be lucidly clear that the challenge that remains for the liturgical movement, following the reform, is liturgical formation. And this seems to me to be the great lesson that recent history has taught us: that we ought to identify ourselves today not so much with our venerated fathers of the Council but with our grandfathers and great-grandfathers from the beginning of the twentieth century. Our faithfulness is not measured so much in the faith that is found in our children, but in what is possible to our grandchildren and great-grandchildren. It will be with them and for them that we have acted, to them and with them that we must ask forgiveness in advance. We must think about these grandparents and these grandchildren and hold ourselves accountable to them. Only in this way will we avoid the despair that comes with fear of what is new and the presumption that results from avoiding what is old, turning instead to the hope that is necessary for each generation to live with the awareness that every era lives *"ummittelbar vor Gott*," immediately before the eyes of God, and for so to respond both according to what is has received and what it passes on.

Each generation—as the poet Wisława Szymborska wrote—"arrives here improvised," and each generation "leaves without the chance to practice." The church, which celebrates the mystery of God the Father, Son, and Holy Spirit, can never forget this difficult truth. Although the initial ignorance and final unpreparedness is an experience that is hard to bear, still it shines luminously and modestly, in the hopeful anticipation of an obedience without despair and a freedom without presumption.